WANDERING IN ANDALUSIA
THE SOUL OF SOUTHERN SPAIN

Other Wanderland Writers Anthologies

WANDERING IN ANDALUSIA
THE SOUL OF SOUTHERN SPAIN

Edited by
Linda Watanabe McFerrin &
Joanna Biggar

Wanderland Writers
Oakland, California

For permission to print essays in this volume, grateful acknowledgement is made to the holders of copyright named on pages 222-231.

Translation of Federico García Lorca's *Procession* from Spanish to English © 2010 by Richard Gard reprinted with kind permission from the translator.

Photographs
Front and back covers:
Front cover, editor photo © Laurie McAndish King
Flamenco dancer © Linda Watanabe McFerrin

Interior photos:
© Rita Gardner 116, 120; © Laurie McAndish King and Jim Shubin vi, xiv, 22, 38, 46, 58, 70, 80, 88, 96, 104, 108, 126, 136, 158; © Jack Martin 202; © Linda Watanabe McFerrin 30, 178; © MJ Pramik 148; © Anne Sigmon 52; © Maryly Snow 184.

Cover design, interior design and map by Jim Shubin, Shubin Design (www.shubindesign.com)
Typefaces: Sabon and Garamond

CATALOGING DATA:
Wandering in Andalusia: The Soul of Southern Spain
Edited by Linda Watanabe McFerrin and Joanna Biggar

ISBN: 978-0-9977054-7-8

First Printing 2016
Printed in the United States of America

For the people of Andalusia

who opened their hearts and homes to us …

Andalusian Balcony

Contents

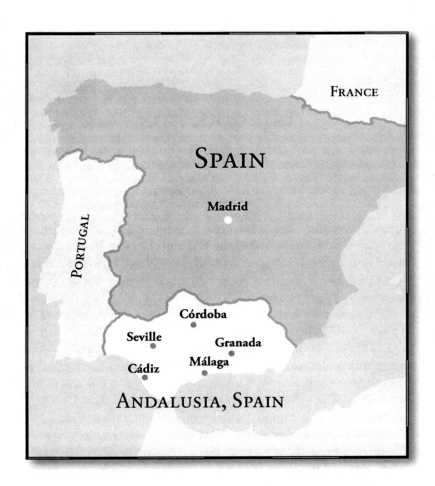

INTRODUCTION

As we stood in the Catedral de Sevilla, before the bones of Columbus, we felt staggered by the scope of time, space and history. Exploration opens up worlds. Those exchanges—the interaction, the wealth of the New World—transformed the Old and the New. In many ways travel does the same thing for an individual. New discoveries change us and we, like Columbus, for good or evil, change the worlds we travel to.

Our reasons for coming to Andalusia differed. Linda returned to a place recently discovered, one that captured the drama and intensity of El Cid; of Cervantes; of modern troubadour, Jim Morrison—the epics, romances and songs that colored her youth. Joanna came in pursuit of a vision refracted from dreams of a long-ago visit and found reflections of her childhood home. We both knew that this was a place we wanted to explore further with our writers and readers.

In many ways, Andalusia, situated as it is, at the southern boundary of the Iberian Peninsula, is a crossroads, a caravansary where settlers from northern Europe, Africa, the Mediterranean and the Middle East have left their mark. A critical center of Roman influence for centuries, the seat of Muslim power for over 800 years, and an early stronghold of Christianity, it has been pivotal in the development of Western culture. Exotic, romantic, alluring, poetic and intense, it is flamenco, *duende*, music, gypsies, guitars, tapas, sherry, sangria, *alegría, muerte*, and lots and lots of ham. Hospitality, *Mudéjar*, gardens, courtyards, bulls, *toreros*, the scent of orange blossoms, civil war and inquisition all factor into the character of the region. Christianity, Islam and Judaism, churches, compassion and sanctity, light and darkness color its magical terrain.

Our writers went from Córdoba to Málaga, from Granada and its Alhambra, to Cádiz to bring back stories of cities, rivers, coasts, plains, food, spirit and passion. Some of our writers took on easy tasks like covering themselves in chocolate or sampling the sherries of Jerez. Others took a more challenging road, following the long *pasos* through the darkened streets of Seville, delving deep into the soul through *duende* or living in a chicken coop. All embarked upon new roads of discovery, and all were well rewarded in their investigations. These, after all, are the landscapes that inspired Cervantes, Lorca, Machado, Navarro, Unamuno, Hemingway, Conrad and Menocal.

But always we came back to Seville and the graceful rooms and courtyards of the Casa Imperial, our home in the heart of the city that was central to our explorations. We have never felt more welcomed and well cared for and we are grateful, as always, for the generosity of spirit in all we encountered.

We invite you, our readers, to visit Andalusia with us through this collection of travel tales, of course, and after that, in your own journeys.

In the words of poet and rock idol, Jim Morrison, "Andalusia with fields ripe with grain, I want to see you again and again."

Linda Watanabe McFerrin and Joanna Biggar
Oakland, California

FOREWORD

Most of us can tell of meeting someone returned recently from travels, and finding them changed. Now and again, it seems as if the change is so thoroughgoing, we have the uncanny sensation that we are talking to someone whose life has taken on an entirely new trajectory.

This happens, because of the power of the places they visit. And to a remarkable degree, such transformations are especially frequent in visitors to Andalusia.

Why is this so? Because what we find in Andalusia cannot be found anywhere else on earth. First of all, the land, cities, and villages there are lustrous with the history of the *convivencia*: the legendary period of the Middle Ages on the Iberian peninsula when Muslims, Christians, and Jews lived and learned together. From them, we have a heritage of wonders: translations of the great philosophers, mathematicians, doctors, and scientists of classical Greece, India, and the Arab world, whose work provided the foundation for the European Renaissance and Enlightenment. We have their architecture of uncanny and potent beauty: the Alhambra in Granada, the Alcázar in Sevilla, the Mezquita in Córdoba, Santa María la Blanca in Toledo—and this is to name but a few. We have musical traditions so complex and powerful that they have survived nearly a millennium—the music of Andalusia is, in fact, the oldest continuously performed genre of music in the world. When we listen to flamenco singing, in all its raw, fierce, uncompromised power, we come into contact with a music so deep in history, and so deep in the mind, that it could not be killed.

And beyond all these splendors, we have a culture of poetry and a spiritual legacy that illuminated the past and brings to the present a light that speaks to our dreams and our longing. The great Jewish and Arab poets of Al-Andalus, the mystical essays of Santa Teresa and radiant poetry of Saint John of the Cross, the poetry and novellas and stories of the Sufis, the verse and theater of Federico Garcia Lorca ... Andalusia is a place where the work of the soul finds a home; where the sensual and the transcendental come together; where experience levers open our understanding, remakes our ideas and hopes, and we see with new vision where prayer and song and stories might lead us.

To change ourselves, we must give ourselves away. The glass we hold cannot be filled until it is first emptied. In Andalusia, we yield ourselves to an irresistible and cumulative beauty, just as we do in love. And the life we then can lead, with reborn and unbound hopes, follows a trajectory of dedication and understanding.

—Steven Nightingale
Author of *Granada: A Pomegranate in the Hand of God* and *The Hot Climate of Promises and Grace.*

Courtyard at the Alhambra

COURTYARDS OF THE CALIPHATE

Joanna Biggar

I did not come to Spain in search of roots. As best I know, my roots lie in Europe far to the north, before my people migrated to California. I certainly did not come seeking the Caliphate—a word that in our times conjures fear, intolerance and death, in ways similar to other words of our past and present: Crusades, Inquisition, jihad. I did come to Spain, to Andalusia, seeking fragments of memories from a trip many decades before, memories like a dream in which courtyards with fountains, flowers, pools and graceful arches open from one to the next evoking mystery, secrets, love. I left having found what I sought—and what I did not know I was seeking.

In Southern California where I was born, the flags of Spain and Mexico had once flown. But (much to my shame now) I never learned their language, and studied little of the culture that my own Anglo one was built upon. In school I learned erroneously, as my parents had, that brave and kindly Spanish monks founded missions and brought gifts of culture and Christianity to grateful Native Americans. I took for granted that I lived in a state with *arroyos, cañóns, patios, ranchos* inside the large embrace of Los Angeles; that my land was dry and filled with palm and orange trees; that it was bordered by deserts, coastal ranges and the sea; and that we liked to visit more distant,

1

snow-capped mountains named the Sierra Nevada. Of course it did not occur to me that just as my culture was created on the foundation of a Spanish one, so the Spanish culture—especially in Andalusia—was built upon a Moorish one.

But by first entering the dream-state of my desires when stepping into the Hotel Casa Imperial in Seville, my awareness, still unconscious, began. Drifting from one courtyard unfolding into the next, I followed tiled paths beneath perfumed orange trees through arcades painted terra cotta, rose, and burnt yellow into another; this one lined with alcoves and flowering geraniums, surrounding a singing fountain. Long-buried memories sprang to life. As if one courtyard answered a distant longing but conjured another, at last I reached the final, most intimate space. There, by the mesmerizing green pool where water trickled melodically all day and night, I sat to contemplate. My previous trip came back to me in vivid focus—its intimations of young love in this passionate city, the intoxicating exoticness of its Moorish design. Oddly, I also felt an unsettling sense of the familiar.

The hotel is said to have been commissioned in the early 1500s by the Marquis de Tarifa, who also built the sumptuous private home, la Casa de Pilotes, a stone's throw away. In both I could see the work of the same artists and craftsmen, making dizzyingly beautiful walls, floors and staircases of intricate tilework—patterns of contrasting blues, greens, golds and browns—in *Mudéjar* style. That style, I learned, came from the Muslims who practiced their own faith without converting as Spain reverted to Christianity. In an age of great tolerance and cultural blending, the *Mudéjar* style was also commonly adapted by Christians and Jews. In la Casa de Pilotes, Christian owners had added a beautiful chapel and religious details to traditional design. Drawn to flowers, tile patterns, water gardens and its enticing courtyards, again I had the sensation of familiarity.

2

But another, older foundation of Islamic culture lies beneath the elaborate *Mudéjar* era. In Córdoba, its avenues ripe with pungent orange trees and its gentle plains rolling green after spring rains, I first encountered it and the Andalusian sensibility of deserts, embedded in Córdoba's very bones.

The Mezquita, now a Catholic cathedral and a UNESCO World Heritage Site, is the centerpiece of the city's history. A mosque built atop a Visigoth church in the eighth century during the reign of Abd ar-Rahman I, the first Caliph of Córdoba, it was expanded and embellished to the end of the tenth century. Then, in the twelfth century, it was reclaimed as a Christian church. Remarkably, instead of destroying the Moorish structure to build anew over it, the Christian rulers were so awed by its beauty that the church became embedded *inside* the mosque's cascading horseshoe-shaped arches.

Made of marble and stone in an alternating red and white striped pattern, I found them hypnotizing. More than any other feature of the great Mezquita, these arches—like courtyards—drew me into and through them in a kind of trance. When I read a description by the twentieth-century Pakistani philosopher and poet, Allama Muhammad Igbal, I understood. The "countless pillars [are]," he said, "like rows of palm trees in the oases of Syria."

Palm trees. Of course. The architects of the caliphate wished to pay homage to their roots in Syria and its deserts. But they were also paying homage to my own. I suddenly envisioned walking hand-in-hand with my grandfather in the evening sunset around the block where we lived, entranced at every step by rows of tall, swaying palms that guarded us like sentinels. I could see the shifting dunes lined with date palms in the deserts around Indio, where we had visited the Date Festival. I remembered a road sign pointing to the town of Mecca.

3

Soon I visited Madinat al-Zahra. Built eight miles west of Córdoba on a plain at the base of the Sierra Morena by Caliph Abd-ar-Rahman III, it was meant to reflect the greatest power in the Islamic world, the Caliphate of Córdoba. Modern art critics have called it the Versailles of the Middle Ages. Construction began in 936 and continued for years until it became a complex of unimaginable splendor including halls, mosques, gardens, palaces and administrative offices, making it the de facto capital of al-Andalus. It is not known if the legend that it was named for the caliph's favorite concubine, al-Zahra, is true—and that she, homesick for Syria, inspired planting many of its flowering fruit trees to imitate flakes descending from snow-capped mountains.

But what is known is that the reign of this brilliant city was short. The Caliphate, first weakened from the inside by a rival faction, was definitively destroyed with the sacking of the city in 1010 by militant Berbers. It lay in ruins for 1,000 years. Only in 1910 did reconstruction begin and is now just 10 percent complete.

Yet for me, incompleteness held its magic. I could sit near the top of the hill and view the outline of its many parts as they tumbled to the plain. I could see the resurrected arches in the red and white motif of the Mezquita evoking rows of palm trees, the intricate wall design of the House of Ya'Far, the grandeur of the caliph's reception hall. Even better, in my imagination I could fill in what was missing. At the most distant reach I could see the outlines of a small yard with a palm tree swaying in the breeze, next to a patch of green. The walls were missing, but I knew that building suites of rooms to surround a small garden—a courtyard—had been invented here and the style was so popular, it rapidly spread throughout all Western Islamic cultures. I imagined al-Zahra's rooms: the floors inlaid with tiles, the intimate courtyard filled with a fountain and arabesques of water;

4

gardens and blossoming trees, watched over by dancing palms.

I tried to conjure what my ancestors were doing in the tenth century, but could only guess. Carrying out rituals around giant stones, perhaps, or tending flocks in rocky fields while living in rude huts—whatever it was, I always felt them very far away. But here, in distant Andalusia, I felt a connection. Deserts, courtyards, palm trees, fountains and an arid kind of mysticism. I could remember warm Christmas days in California sitting on a patio and thinking with skepticism about white Christmases with mistletoe and forest elves, while the pictures in my children's Bible showed sand, men dressed in robes and sandals, palm trees—like the soil beneath my city, like the shoes worn on its streets, like the trees in my neighborhood.

Those connections became less opaque when, at last, I traveled to Granada's fabled Alhambra. There, leaning against a wall and looking across to the old Moorish town of Albaicín, I saw a tower, rectangular in shape with a gently sloping tile-covered roof, and did a double-take. It was an exact copy of a tower in my junior high school. Or a forebear, to be precise.

Then, contemplating the extravagant, disorienting style of the fourteenth-century Nasrid Palaces, the last burst of Moorish royal architecture in Spain, I found myself mesmerized by the Room of the Two Sisters. Its semi-circular arched entrances overlapped with layers of hanging filigree, which sometimes, the writer María Rosa Menocal suggests, resemble stalactites. The walls, in patterns of intricate swirls like lace, drew my eye forward, across the tiled interior to the smaller arches overlooking a garden. And there I had another moment of déjà vu—the busy-ness of hanging colonnades, the complicated swirls over massive arches, the heady perfume of the garden, the sound of water—I recognized these, features of the Mission Inn in Riverside, where I had danced under the stars at college proms.

My past came into focus more clearly. The world I had grown up with was so like Andalusia not only in its arid climate, coastline, orange groves and snowy mountains, but also in its architecture and culture. I had absorbed these unconsciously. I had been surrounded by Spanish words, place names, ideas. My great-aunt once inhabited a historic Spanish adobe landmark. I had lived not far from the San Gabriel Mission, and Spanish clay pipes bringing water from a mill to the mission passed near the roots of our enormous oak tree, watering it during times of drought. My house had features similar to so many I had seen in Spain, with white-washed walls, a red tile roof, a tiled double-story hall with a curved staircase and wrought-iron railing.

But beneath the Spanish exterior, I could now see the Moorish influence I had also grown up with, much of it due to an explosion of the Spanish and Moorish Revival movement in the 1920s and '30s. There were extravagant Hollywood houses with their *Mudéjar* tilework and patios; exotic "Moorish" domes that adorned theaters and hotels; intimate, enclosed gardens with seductive trills of trickling water. Some of these, like the Alhambra itself, were fanciful and lavish public buildings, such as William Randolph Hearst's San Simeon castle on the Central California coast. Its mishmash of styles incorporated many *Mudéjar* features, including the Casa del Sol guesthouse with a tile courtyard, an elaborate gold-worked main door, and flowering vines clinging to slender archways. Designed by famed architect Julia Morgan, its style was called Moorish. I encountered these features in smaller, more intimate spaces, too. There were the Andalusia Apartments on Sunset Boulevard, with their charming balconies and pots of geraniums overhanging courtyards, such as I had seen in Córdoba. There was the long, Moroccan-tiled pool in a hidden garden, such as I had seen in Seville, where I used to seek solitude at Scripps College. There was my own house, with its winding staircase and fancy tilework.

But these features of the *Mudéjar* period were not the only homages to the Moors I found in my homeland. References to the old order, from the days of the Caliphate exist too. There are buildings such as the Shrine Auditorium in Los Angeles that looks like a desert palace surrounded by palm trees; there are mortuaries with red and white striped archways that recall the Mezquita; there are courtyards themselves, a gift from the splendid Madinat al-Zahra during the reign of Caliph Abd ar Rahman III.

In school I had learned, as every American child does, that 1492 was a very important year. It was the year that Columbus "discovered" America—and also the year that the Catholic Monarchs Ferdinand and Isabella expelled the Jews and the last Moors from Spain. But did they?

My passage through the courtyards of the Casa Imperial had in the end revealed a secret, and my passage through Andalusia had yielded another story. The Moors, with their high culture, their learning and refinement, their legacy embodied in the most splendid cities, structures and design, appeared to be everywhere. It seemed to me they had never left.

Not only that. Of all the things for good or ill that came with Columbus's voyages to the New World, I discovered another dimension. In his wake came Spanish rule and a way of life that would be the foundation of California. Embedded in that culture were the seeds of Islamic Spain that would implant in fertile California soil and flourish again. No wonder I found roots in Andalusia: In some measure I had grown up there.

Two Women at a Window, by Bartolomé Esteban Murillo

Two Women at a Window

Sandra Bracken

*—After a painting by Bartolomé Esteban Murillo,
painted between 1655 and 1660 in Seville*

I've been waiting
for orange blossoms to
scent the air.
Waiting here in Jardines Murillo
remembering when I first saw you
so many years ago.

Your eyes found mine, held my gaze;
your smile easy and warm
and welcoming.
I stopped in expectation
presuming you would speak—
that you could speak.
Your left arm rested on the windowsill,
your right hand under your chin—

a proud, relaxed pose—
your hair, shiny, pulled neatly up and back,
your face flush with sunlight.
I noticed the very small crimson flower
tucked in your bodice,
another behind your ear.
What were you doing there?
I think it was not simply to take in the view.
Perhaps there's an answer from the woman
standing in the shadows
very near but behind you.
In an impulsive gesture, she
pulled her scarf to her face.
Shy perhaps
but she could not hide
the delight in her eyes, her
enthusiasm for that shared moment.
What did she, breathless, whisper to you—
you, so calm, poised?

Was she one who easily
indulges her imagination?
Maybe she thought
she could not be seen
in the darkness of the room—
her hand on the wooden shutter.
Holding it open?
Or preparing to close it?
But I think neither of you
would leave the window.

I could see that you were
comfortable in each other's company.
Sisters? Friends?
In seventeenth century Spain, in Seville,
perhaps one of you was the duenna?
I felt the easiness between you
that you knew what the other was thinking.
But neither of you revealed the focus
of your attention.
I wondered, were you a picture of
expectation?
Or one of certainty?
Or was it waiting that you did best?

I wanted to be invited in. Surely
there was space in that darkened corner
where
I could sit in silence
and listen,
wanting to hear as you did
the sounds drifting in
from Calle Santa Teresa.
I wanted to discover what brought you there
to the window just then.
Perhaps it was simply a private moment.
Perhaps it was a daily habit, the time
when you shared the gossip of the day.
I couldn't help feeling
that you were waiting
for someone.

And I would never know
unless I could wait with you.

A heady sweetness fills the air
as the day grows warmer in the park.
Ageless trees temper the sounds of
doves cooing and courting,
children playing and
tourists gathering on tiled benches
momentarily, then moving on.
A gray tabby takes their place.
Stately columns stand empty,
their capitals on the ground nearby—
evidence of the past.
My thoughts wander to your street
so close.

A handsome young man
enters the park
—dark eyes and hair curling toward his face—
tall, shoulders back,
the countenance of a dancer.
A secret smile fills the corners of his mouth.
Walking toward Plaza Santa Cruz his
measured steps quicken,
become hurried
with a purpose.
I wonder,
will he pause by your window
look up
and smile?

Matador Curro Diaz

ON DEATH AND BULLS

Linda Watanabe McFerrin

I fought my first bull when I was sixteen. In the middle of the small but beautiful arena in Texcoco, Mexico, standing alone and unprotected under the intense noonday sun, I faced my adversary while the well-heeled lunch crowd cheered me on.

Even then I knew something about bullfighting. A romantic kid with a passion for travel, I had already read Ernest Hemingway's *Death in the Afternoon* and *The Matador*, a book that Barnaby Conrad, one of my uncle's literary pals and a forty-seven-time matador had written about the *corrida de toros* ... but these were remote fantasies based on the exploits of brave old men. I could never have imagined I'd ever be physically involved in an art form in three acts that end in death—one that Hemingway famously called not a sport, but a tragedy.

But there I stood, living the dream in my extra-short red dress and fashionable sandals, my pinkish bullfighting cape held in preparation for a *molinete* or *verónica*, seemingly simple passes that can be executed without looking too uncoordinated. I stood my ground. The animal charged.

Did I mention that I was on an un-chaperoned nine-day field trip to Mexico financed largely by the accommodating but unquestionably careless parents of our group of six teenage girls?

At the last minute our male Spanish teacher had very wisely decided not to accompany us on this journey. Did I also mention that it was a baby bull? At La Morena, back in the day, foolish restaurant- and bar-goers could sign up for the ring, thereby providing an afternoon of amusement for the assembled. Sometimes they were injured, like the New York cosmetics industry entrepreneur who broke a wrist during her performance. I, on the other hand, managed to acquit myself reasonably well. I did not run, as one of my classmates who also opted to brave the day's ultra-amateur *becerrada* did.

Running, we discovered, is never a good idea. The bull chases you, and even if the *toreros* manage to distract it, you end up on the ground—as my friend did, much to her eternal mortification—with your too-short skirt up over your head and your face in the sand. This was not the case during my performance. A cheer rose up from the crowd as my cape swept the floor of the arena. I managed a couple of clumsy passes before the increasingly nervous and extraordinarily handsome professional *toreadors* stepped in, quickly diverting the animal and congratulating me on my minor accomplishment. From that debut moment, and for quite some time afterwards, I was hooked on bullfights.

It was, however, downhill after that. I did attend other *corridas* when I managed to get back to Mexico, not as a participant but as a spectator. I discovered that the art form is not always graceful and heroic. If a bullfight is good, it's a beautiful, highly stylized battle between man and beast, one that the human does not necessarily win, especially if the two are well matched. If it isn't good, it's a messy slaughter, usually of the beasts—the bulls and the horses. Unfortunately, this is often the case, which is one of the reasons bull-fighting is so despised. At its best, it is a ritual of some magnificence, a sacrifice in which the participants—matadors, *banderilleros, peones, picadors*, bulls, horses—are all supposed to behave bravely in the most importunate of spectacles, "the only place," claimed Hemingway, "that you could see life and death, i.e., violent death now that the wars were over …."

In Andalusia, the bullfighting tradition, which probably has its roots in prehistoric bull worship and sacrifice in ancient Mesopotamia, is still very much alive. This is not so all over Spain. In Spain's autonomous community of Catalonia, for example, it is illegal, having been banned in 2010, ostensibly over concerns about animal welfare, although some think that this happened more because of the people—Catalan separatism, and a desire, perhaps, to distinguish themselves from their countrymen—than for the sake of the bulls. But in Andalusia, where gigantic black Osborne bulls still reign over the rural hills—even though the advertising slogans to which they were once devoted were banned—bullfighting is still a proud tradition. There are, in fact, thousands of bullfights in Spain every year, many of them connected with the fairs and fiestas of the great cities of Andalusia as well as in Spain's capital city and its many provinces. The *corrida* is as Spanish as flamenco or tapas or the Spanish guitar, part of Iberian culture since 711 and an official feature at celebrations since the coronation of King Alfonso VIII in 1133.

Today it is a performance perfected over centuries, a death ritual in which all the human participants at risk are complicit. It unfolds in three acts: the *Tercio de Veras*, in which the bull and matador meet; the *Tercio de Banderillas*, during which the bull is further provoked by men on horseback; and the *Tercio de Muerte*, when the bull is killed. Over the years, the spectacle has changed significantly. In a more courtly time, bullfights took place mainly on horseback and were a privilege of social position. The *Tercio de Banderillas* reflects this older form, the *rejoneando*, introduced by the Moors who prided themselves on their horsemanship. Riders still have their place in modern bullfights, but the matador on foot, the "everyman," has been the hero since 1726 when Francisco Romero, a commoner from the Andalusian town of Ronda, and others like him, revolutionized the presentation and became Spain's first wildly successful professional matadors.

In Seville, in the days preceding *Semana Santa*, I find the symbol of the bull as prevalent as the Christ: Christ in the streets and in the churches. Bulls in the ring and in the restaurants and bars. This is the bullfight season and in the eating and drinking establishments around the Triana near the big yellow Plaza de Toros de la Maestranza on Paseo de Colon and in the heart of Seville, I sit with friends and drink sangria and Spanish wines and eat tapas under the severed and stuffed heads of heroic bulls, and contemplate the nature of sacrifice, its brutality and the way we glorify and ritualize it—a subject hard to ignore in these days before Holy Week begins.

I have friends who find the bullfights cruel and immoral. I can understand the concern for the animals' plight, but that doesn't mean I can fathom the basis of their opposition, particularly if they consume animal flesh and aren't fastidious about the way those animals have been slaughtered. Have they read Upton Sinclair? Have they heard about Temple Grandin? Do they know that the bulls that fight in *corridas* are a unique breed of cattle, the *toro de lidia*, famous for its aggressive behavior and raised especially for the purpose; that they must weigh at least 410 kg to fight anywhere and be over four years old? These animals mature on vast ranches or *dehesas*— essentially wildlife habitats—in conditions far superior to those of cattle raised for meat, which lead short and confined lives, rarely more than eighteen months. And while I can count on one hand the times I've consumed red meat in the years since college, I'm not going to bust anyone's chops for consuming a chop, particularly if that person is cognizant of their part in the drama of death that surrounds our survival. I grew up in a world where hunting and fishing were perfectly acceptable ways of delivering food to the table. If you kill it and dress it and eat it, you are partaking in a life ritual that is as old as time and as sacred. What I love about Spain is that ethos still exists, especially in Andalusia, in places like Antequera where inns like Restaurante-Hotel Venta las Delicias still pay homage to the animals that end up on the table.

At Pepe Hillo in Seville, a tapas bar named after Jose Delgado Guerra, one of Spain's most illustrious matadors, I savor the convivial vibe and admire the bullfighting memorabilia. I have not visited the bullring in Seville, and feel that I am in some way abandoning the romance of earlier days. I wonder if along with my youthful passion for the *corrida*, I have given up hope. The bulls and the matadors do represent courage, at least to me, and I worry that with age and a history of lost loved ones and tragic deaths, I may have lost that earlier strength.

It's raining when my friends and I get to Ronda, a mountain town famous for the *corrida*. We explore for a bit then duck into a restaurant across from the bullring. Inspired by the upcoming holiday, I uncharacteristically order goat, a food that our friend Thanasis says is often associated with Greek Easter. I've dined exclusively on fish and fowl for decades. The goat is delicious.

In the back of the restaurant is a room filled with the images of bullfighters, the bullrings and the bulls. I feel as if I'm in a shrine, a place that glows with the same energy and exhilaration I felt when I was a teen: Antonio Ordonez, Pedro Romero, the exquisite Cristina Sanchez, and more. The rain abates and we step outside into the sunshine to explore Ronda. Later, when the clouds part and the rain stops, we return to the bullring where I stand in front of the statue of Cayetano Ordonez y Aguilera aka Nino de Palma, renowned for his success in Ronda and Seville, and model for Ernest Hemingway's Pedro Romano. The posture, sweep of the cape, the commitment and sublime dedication to the moment at hand that emanate from the artwork all move me profoundly. I am transported to my own childhood perhaps, to a hero-populated, far simpler and clearer place and time. My friends are moving on. I know we are leaving, but before we go I reach out to the bronze figure to touch it in the way a matador might touch the shoulder of the bull in delivering the final *estocada* ... in kinship, in respect, in gratitude, in reverence.

Jamón

JAMÓN PILGRIMAGE

Sandra Bracken

When Alberto said, "an Iberian pig is like a walking olive tree," I stopped and listened more closely. He was pointing out one of the characteristics that makes *jamón Ibérico de bellota* so special: the fat consists of approximately fifty-five percent oleic acid, making it full of antioxidants—a healthy fat! By the end of the tour, I'd begun to understand why the Spanish ham Alberto was talking about was quite unlike the ham produced on my grandparents' farm in Virginia. I knew that the story was not so simple as feeding acorns to pigs. My quest was just beginning in the Sierra de Aracena west of Seville. Later that day on a *finca* (farm), I spent an afternoon with Elena and her parents who proudly explained the subtleties of the life of the black-footed pig. There I realized that it could be true, that diet and exercise can make a big difference, even for a pig.

My interest in how a pig becomes a ham began at an early age. It was part of the adventure and mystery associated with my grandparents' farm, along with other conundrums like how their wheat became bread and how corn was transformed into muffins. Unlike our food in the city, which was purchased mostly in markets, their food came from their gardens, fields and from the animals they raised on their acreage in central Virginia. This was a pragmatic decision for them, not a philosophical one. How grown up I felt being put to work as a farmhand during my visits! Feeding the pigs was one of the chores I was assigned. Those massive black creatures spent their days in a large enclosed field and knew just when to come to the trough for meals. In addition to grains, they were also fed our table scraps and cooking leftovers. While I thought that was a generous idea, carrying and emptying the slop bucket was not my favorite job. I understood its necessity in the same way I accepted the bleeding out of the recently slaughtered pigs, the butchering and the preparation for the curing process. I knew the end result would be that special aroma coming from the smoke house—and eventually, what I had anxiously been waiting for: that thin but oh-so-tasty slice of ham tucked into one of grandmother's hot biscuits.

My grandparents' good quality free-range country-cured ham is now a memory. I've always wanted to carry on the tradition of serving it to my family just as my mother had, but its scarcity surprised me. This led to some research. That's how I became familiar with Spanish ham, especially *jámon Ibérico de bellota* and made my decision to visit some *pata negra* (black-footed *Ibérian*) pigs. So when the opportunity arose to join a writing workshop in Andalusia, I signed up, hoping to learn more about the cured ham that is regarded as the world's very best. *Jámon Ibérico de bellota* (*bellota* is Spanish for acorns) comes from an ancient breed of pigs found only in southwestern Spain. I was not going to explore the origins of other types of Spanish hams like *jámon Ibérico*, which, although it also comes from the *pata negra* breed, for one reason or another, doesn't meet the standard. *Serrano*, a popular Spanish ham from a different breed of pig, has a different diet with a shorter aging period. Other countries in Europe produce fine ham; Parma and Prosciutto ham in Italy, Bigorre ham in France, Black Forest in Germany. In the United States, the only comparable ham product is known as country ham or Virginia ham because of its origin. It is similar to my grandparents' ham. However, *jamón Ibérico de bellota* is universally recognized as the finest ham anywhere.

Before leaving, I contacted A Taste of Spain, the company that organized my day trip and driver to the Sierra de Aracena just west of Seville. The drive was a gradual, easy rise to and through the *dehesa,* a mix of grasslands and forests. In Jabugo, I visited the showroom and production facility of Cinco Jotas. We parked next to a gleaming white building and entered an elegant showroom where their products were displayed in fine wood and glass showcases. Alberto, my guide, graciously led me through a lovely historical building, talking easily about the company, which was founded in 1879. Banners highlighting their tradition hung in the open courtyard graced with an appealing sculpture of a sow and two piglets. In other rooms we found clever displays with additional information, particularly on the salting process. All the while Alberto answered my many questions. The last area we visited was an awesomely large, antiseptically clean space—the aging room—where hundreds of hams hung. Cinco Jotas hams cure for three to four years. My appetite was already sufficiently stimulated when Alberto set out a plate of *jamón*—thinly shaved bite-sized pieces, dark red, and glistening— along with *picos comperos* (small bread sticks) and a glass of chilled *fino* sherry. A terrific beginning to my research.

Our next stop was Finca Montefrio, where delightful Elena, daughter of owners Loli and Armando, met me. While we strolled under the ancient oaks she talked enthusiastically about the family's organic farm. At one point, we were surrounded by an energetic group of lean black pigs, one daring to take a taste of my espadrilles. Elena described their herd's day: On waking the pigs climb high up on the property, coming back for food and a siesta later, before repeating the same routine. She also explained in some detail the foods and feeding schedule on their farm. The piglets get started on the sow's milk. As they grow they are fed special organic grains for a time, then later while exploring the *dehesa*, they feast on the ground crops like clover, green pea plants and margarita flowers planted just for them. When they are about two years old, in the last six months of their lives, they gorge solely on acorns. It's that acorn diet at that specific time that produces the distinctive fat that runs through the pigs muscles and meat.

Armando, Elena's father, took me to their aging room, significantly smaller than the one at *Cinco Jotas*, where less than a hundred hams were hanging. Later he demonstrated the proper way to slice a ham. When he handed me the knife, I found it was not easy, even though I was using the proper flexible thin bladed tool, and the ham was secured in the traditional stand. Meanwhile, Loli, Elena's mother, had prepared a generous gourmet luncheon using only products from their farm—set at a table by an open fire: appetizers of paté, chorizo sausage, *jamón Ibérico de bellota,* blood sausage with tomatoes, then a squash soup followed by a piece of grilled pork loin, or *lomo,* served with a salad and finally dessert—a custard with cinnamon sprinkled on top. All of this was accompanied by a fine local Spanish wine. What was so incredibly enjoyable was being with a family, seeing how conscientiously they cared for their pigs and their farm, creating both a lifestyle and a livelihood. As the afternoon came to an end I couldn't help but feel grateful that they had chosen to share it.

What I learned that day is that basically all you need to create a dry cured ham is salt and air and time. That sounds simple enough, but there are many variations in each step that are reflected in the taste and texture. Much was said by my hosts about the importance of the perfect cool temperatures in the mountains around Jabugo; about the humidity and how they naturally regulate those elements during the aging process by opening and closing windows or putting water on the floor of the aging room. While they adhere to an ancient way of doing things, to ensure a consistent product the process is highly regulated by the government. For example an Iberian *pata negra* pig must have two hectares (approximately five acres) of space in which to roam. After the "sacrifice" and butchering, the raw meat is covered in sea salt for a week or two then washed. There's a settling stage, then hams are hung in a drying room for up to six months before going into an aging room. The acorn diet produces the healthy fat and so much daily exercise forces the fat into the muscles of the pig. The layering of fat makes it possible for them to be cured much longer, resulting in a more complex, intense flavor: A slice of ham marbled with a yellowish fat that practically melts at room temperature, melts in your mouth.

Whether it is *Ibérico de bellota, Ibérico* or *Serrano,* Spaniards are proud of their ham. It's everywhere: hanging in groups in the markets and on every bar in every tapas restaurant, displayed in the traditional ham-holding stand or sitting out on counters, ready for the next slice. I read an article entitled "The world's best ham: it may be $150/pound but it may be worth it." An online search showed that Cinco Jotas whole hams are now available in the United States for approximately $1,000 per ham. Cost varies depending on the cut— shoulder or hind leg, sixteen to seventeen pounds. I discovered ham tastings, described in much the same way as wine tastings are. I also saw an organic Finca Montefrio ham advertised, although not available in the United States. Too bad. Someone asked me if the Cinco Jotas ham was worth the cost. Of course the only answer to that question is, "Try it, decide for yourself."

After ten days in Andalusia eating *jamón Ibérico* and *jamón Ibérico de bellota* in tapas bars, bodegas, hotels, restaurants and a farmhouse dining room, I feel I've at last made up for years of deprivation. I'm liking the over-indulgence and am feeling not a bit guilty, knowing what a healthful experience it has been.

Although there's little resemblance to the ham I learned to love as a child, I am reminded of my grandparents, who introduced me to the pleasures of cured ham and who, in many ways, lived a life similar to that on Finca Montefrio. I was on a singular mission when I went to Spain. In looking for one thing, I encountered something more. I reconnected with a traditional way of life that I will remember every time I taste *jamón de bellota*. I'll be back in the *dehesa* on a cool spring day walking through clover and daisies with a feeling that all's well in my world.

Tapas Server at Il Rinconcillo

Me Gusta Mucho:
SAVORING TAPAS IN SEVILLE

Tania Amochaev

My mind froze. People stared, beer from the spigot overflowed, the noise level increased, the poised woman next to me gently patted her red lips, and the moment stretched painfully . . .

A few years before, my husband and I enjoyed some wonderful modern Spanish cooking in fine restaurants around Barcelona with cosmopolitan maîtres d'hôtel and menus in English. But this time, my first in Seville, gourmet chefs weren't my priority. I wanted to eat like the locals and had diligently listened to my *Learn Spanish in Your Car* tapes in preparation. I was ready . . . until it was time to order in this busy restaurant with no menus, no English, no time for beginners.

Sara, whose family owned the Hotel Casa Imperial, a traditional mansion where I was staying, had recommended Il Rinconcillo, a tapas place just a short walk away. Tapas are small snacks, mostly served at simple bars variously called *cervecerias*, beer pubs, or *bodegas*, wine cellars. I sat down at an outdoor table and indicated the small portion I was interested in.

"*No se puede , señora,*" said the black-vested waiter. "*No aquí.*" At the outdoor tables, he said, I could order only full-sized plates. Seeing

31

my dismay, the man finally took me by the arm and led me away, around the corner. There I found the locals' version of this restaurant, where people crowded and jostled for position at an old bar and waiters wrote running bill totals in chalk directly on its wooden surface. My well-dressed and coiffed neighbor stood elbow to elbow with me, delicately nibbling small fried fish. As the waiter was about to give up on me in disgust, I finally just pointed at her plate. He chalked 2.50 on the counter and sped away. The lady, who I was afraid would scorn my casual hiking attire, smiled and held out her plate to me. "*Le gustará*," she said. "You will like it," an expression with which I was to become familiar. Before I had time to consider taking one, a small plateful of the crispy four-inch-long fried anchovies appeared before me.

She was right; I liked them. From that first bite I was launched on a broad exploration of fried fish, and, in particular, these *boquerone* —anchovies. They were crunchy and tasty, although I did remove a few bones and heads, not yet comfortable chewing through them.

My elegant neighbor then indicated a cloven-hoofed leg of dry ham, which pointed disturbingly at me from the counter. The waiter deftly sliced thin strips of the *jamón Iberico*, which cannot be imported into California—the closest familiar comparison is Italian prosciutto—completing a delectable starter experience in tapas, and making me feel like a pro when I subsequently brought my friends there.

After that first experience there was no stopping me. I ate and talked my way through the town. As my Spanish improved, my conversations became inadvertently funnier. One night, after a flamenco performance, my friend Daphne and I stopped in a tiny, simple neighborhood bodega. She egged me on.

"Say something," she whispered, giggling. We weren't on our first *cerveza*, as beer had been an early and important word to memorize.

I pointed at a large round of oily cheese under glass.

"*Qué es eso?*" I asked the waiter.

"*Queso.*"

"*Qué tipo de queso es?*"

"*Muy bueno. Muy viejo. Le gustará.*"

The truth is, I learned a lot from this nonsensical conversation in which he told me the obvious: that it was cheese, and that it was old and good, and that I would like it. He subsequently told me that it had been aged six months, packed in oil to make it harder and dryer. Importantly, I finally understood that all cheese in simple bodegas was manchego, a firm sheep's milk cheese, and was just called *queso* or cheese. In fact, all the food was simple, prepared as it had been for centuries. No fusion. No experimental juxtapositions. No high prices.

Wanting to complete my notes, I then asked the name of the place.

"*Ah! Es Las Cinco Farolas!*"

The comedic exchange that followed led me to think that *farolas* were the trees in the small square, or the moon, or maybe the streetlamps. Finally the waiter took me outside and pointed to the five lights that lined the front of the bodega. Those were the *cinco farolas*.

Midnight approached; they were anxious to close up, and it was my turn to pay. The bill for two soups, two beers and the cheese was €11.50. The price was similar to that of all the meals I was to have in tapas bars. I quickly realized that joy could be found on the cheap, hidden in the nooks and crannies of Seville.

The next day on my early morning walk I headed out to visit Castillo San Jorge, the monument to the Spanish Inquisition on the banks of the Guadalquivir River. It was still closed, but cases of fresh seafood on ice were being unpacked next door at the Mercado de

Triana. A fishmonger waved some small lobsters at me. "*Le gustará*," he said, but I already knew that. What I didn't know was where I could go eat them. In my improving Spanish I convinced him to share a restaurant that might serve such delicacies. He first mentioned a place where my group had eaten the night before, but immediately told me it was pricey and suggested an alternative. He told me to take the photo I had just snapped of him and his lobsters to Bar El Tremendo, about a mile from the old town center, on Calle Previsión, and show it to the owner. "Tell him Manuel sent you," he added. I couldn't wait to try this insider experience.

On my first walk to El Tremendo, however, an aroma of frying fish distracted me just minutes into my journey. The street-side bar I was passing, La Taberna del Pintor on Calle Valle, had a sign near the door that read: "*Hay albures y cazon en* adobo *mosto del aljarafe*."

The closest I could come to a translation—marinated dogfish in a historic Sevillian wine of some kind—almost drove me away, but I persisted. As I sat on a tall barstool just outside the front door, the owner brought me chunks of fried fish accompanied by large pieces of a giant radish and a small *cerveza*. The first bite had me pulling bones between my teeth and wondering what I had been thinking. But by the final piece I decided it was very unique and exceptionally tasty. A slightly meatier version of the fried anchovies I had in mind, with crunchy skin and a subtle undertaste of pickling. Even with the outside tables, there was room for fewer than fifteen people, and they all knew each other. Irresistible.

Of course I had to return.

"Can I help you, Mum?" I heard upon entering the same place a few days later. This wasn't Spanish emerging from a broad grin behind a red beard. "He told me you'd be back," the bartender continued, winking conspiratorially at the owner. I learned that this transplanted

Irishman normally wrote tech manuals but spent *Semana Santa,* Holy Week, helping his neighborhood bar cope with the crowds that were already pouring in. Ordering didn't require much thought—a portable burner made up the entire kitchen, and fried *adobo* was the single offering—but it was well worth the return trip.

I was still determined to find El Tremendo. Its street, Calle Previsión, is another twenty-minute walk away from the interesting alleys of old Seville. Nestled amidst apartment blocks, it is a single lively strip of tapas places. They are so simple that there is a small bar and a table or two inside each one, and a few plastic tables and chairs on the sidewalk, shared randomly between them. The owner of El Tremendo gave Manuel's photo a large grin and indicated the seafood in the refrigerated case behind him. I pointed, we talked, and I took my *cerveza* outside to see what would show up.

I hit the jackpot. *Cigala a la plancha,* so good it required seconds, translates as grilled Norwegian lobster. It seemed mere hours out of the water. And the tasty *salmonete*—deep-fried little salmon-colored fish that translated to red mullet—could easily be eaten, bones and all.

I was certainly hitting my stride with great food, and alternated sophisticated dinners late at night with rambling culinary explorations by day.

A few days later, the memory of that lobster had me heading back to El Tremendo on the animated street where, I had since learned, Manuel the fishmonger's family lived. It was unfortunately all dark at that spot, for it was Wednesday, the weekly day of closure.

Disappointed, I went two doors down, to a small place on the order of a diner with Spanish tiles, called Cervecería Casa Pepe. Pepe, who looked a lot like Pavarotti without the excess weight, smiled until he had to tell me he couldn't serve the wild asparagus sitting in a jar on the counter until the next day, for it had to be prepared. My pleas went unheard, and he finally offered up *boquerones fritos* instead. Of course I said, "*Sí, con una cerveza pequeña, por favor.*"

The fish that sat on a six-inch plate before me were certainly the smallest legal anchovies, and I swear all the bones had been removed. They were smoothly covered in the lightest dusting of flour and they tasted of the sea, their texture crunchy and soft at the same time. My bites got smaller as the plate emptied. When Pepe asked, "*Le gustará?*" I just grinned and ordered a second, if for no other reason than to memorize the flavors.

By then I had made friends with the buxom blond waitress, and she promised to convince Pepe to make me a wild asparagus, *jamón* and shrimp omelet if I could return that evening. I certainly could.

I enjoyed many more tapas experiences, too many to describe them all, although specific moments keep coming to mind. With Sara, who spent incredible amounts of time telling me the secrets of Seville, I roamed about town tasting her favorite *bacalao con tomate*—salt cod in tomato sauce—looking for one that might approach her grandmother's delicacy. She taught me what she and all her friends knew: You had one tapa and a drink, and then moved on to the next place, maximizing the experience. My friend Linda and I wandered to Pepe Hillo, where I enjoyed what Sara had assured me was the best *solomillo al whiskey*—pork brined in whiskey. Plaza Alfalfa, nearby, had several bodegas that introduced us to an intensity of meat dishes almost unimaginable, represented by tapas that translated to "pork stuffed with pig and sprinkled with bacon bits" and "pig terrine with a touch of foie gras."

I learned it didn't require famous chefs or a lot of money to eat food to remember in Seville. You will not find Bar El Tremendo, Cervecería Casa Pepe, La Taberna del Pintor, or Las Cinco Farolas in the Michelin or any other sophisticated guide to the city. You might hear about Il Rinconcillo, but perhaps not about the back corner stand-up bar where they are too busy serving food to learn English. You will certainly want to try the best restaurants. But if you trust your senses, you just might find joy in exploring the simplest of tapas bars.

As for Spanish? Learn to point, smile, and when you want more, say, "*Me gusta mucho!*"

Spanish Baths

CHOCOTHERAPY

Laurie McAndish King

A young masseuse named Sandra had slathered my body in dark chocolate from neck to toe. The consistency of Hershey's syrup, it slid on, thin and cool, dripping into my armpits, pooling around my bellybutton, and trickling between my toes.

This wasn't what I'd expected when I journeyed to Seville, in the southern part of Spain, during the week before *Semana Santa*. Religious processions, yes. Advance Holy Week celebrations, of course. Wonderful food and wine, surely. But a chocolate massage?

I'd been on the road for nearly twenty-seven hours and wanted to visit a local spa as soon as I arrived, to loosen my airline-induced knots and kinks. I was looking forward to experiencing Seville's own brand of *hammam*, knowing the Andalusian city had retained some of the flavor of its earlier Moorish inhabitants. A traveler has to take life as it comes, though, which is why I ended up lying flat on my back on a marble slab in a dark room, coated in cool, sticky chocolate.

The Arab baths, or *baños Arabes*, were in the Santa Cruz quarter of the city, just a short walk from my hotel. Housed in a sixteenth-century *Mudéjar* palace that the brochure said "maintains the legacy of our *ancestros* who made public baths a treat for the senses," the ancient spa sounded like an ideal way to begin my stay in Seville. The brochure listed an anti-stress massage, which seemed fitting after my long trip. It also included several tempting "rituals," including a "My Perfect Skin Ritual," the geographically authentic-sounding "Al-Andalus Ritual" (whatever that might be), and most promising, something called a "Four-Handed Ritual." I was all in for the four-handed treatment when I spotted something even more enticing: "Thermal Bath + Chocotherapy."

Chocotherapy!

With real chocolate? How was it possible that I'd never heard of this before? And how had I managed to live for decades without experiencing it? Chocotherapy sounded like an essential part of a life well lived; I wasted no time signing up for my session.

They couldn't get me in right away, so I took advantage of the opportunity to enjoy chocolate in the usual way and walked to a nearby "Chocolate and Churros" stand—one of many that dot the streets of Seville, sending their delicious aromas into the soft air to mingle with the scents of jasmine and orange blossoms, garlic and fried fish, and the occasional whiff of diesel. Seville is an olfactory extravaganza.

Although there were plenty of churros on display, the friendly cook made up a fresh batch especially for me, kneading the dough and frying up a tall mound of fluffy little columns of carbohydrate. I tasted a churro first. Exceptionally light and tender, it was almost like eating air—deep-fried, high-calorie air. It was not sweetened and would go perfectly with the glass of chocolate milk. But this was no ordinary glass of chocolate milk. Smooth, velvety, bitter-sweet, more the consistency of a thin pudding than a beverage, it was an adults-only version of everyone's favorite flavor—and exactly right for churros-dipping. One taste explained why the chocolate-and-churros stands were all over the city. So dark and luscious—the stuff was addictive! These Spaniards really knew their chocolate.

And no wonder; I had read that Spain was the birthplace of modern chocolate. Modern chocolate? As compared with ... what? As compared with New World chocolate, the "food of the gods" of the Mayans and of the Aztecs who conquered them. The chocolate that explorer Hernán Cortés de Monroy y Pizarro, Marquis of the Valley of Oaxaca, had stockpiled and sent back to the Spanish crown more than 500 years ago. New World chocolate was ground and mixed with chili peppers, but no sweetener was added. In fact, the word "chocolate" may have come from the Mayan word "*xocolatl*," which actually means "bitter water." It's the Old World Spanish who first thought to add sugar, a treat from the Canary Islands that transformed a spicy, bitter brew into the delicious elixir we know and love today; the irresistible confection that Americans eat twelve pounds of, per person, per year. The Swiss consume nearly twice that much. The stuff would soon be enveloping my entire body.

I arrived at the *baños Arabes*, ready for my chocotherapy experience. First came a long soak in the rooftop spa, where I relaxed in a heated pool and watched the sun sink into a pink sky, illuminating the steeples of a dozen nearby churches. Doves cooed, and the sweet scent of orange blossoms drifted up from the street. Heaven.

Next I was treated to the thermal baths: A comfortable, ninety-seven-degree tepidarium, enhanced with a hydrotherapy device that bubbled so effusively it shot plumes of spray more than a foot above the surface of the water; a hot-tub-like one-hundred-and-four-degree caldarium that drained me of any lingering tension; and a bracing sixty-one-degree frigidarium that tightened my skin into tiny, startled goosebumps.

Each marble-tiled pool was in its own room, long and quiet, except for the burble and splash of water, and the occasional low murmur of other bathers. Masses of candles flickering through delicate cages illuminated ancient brick walls and high ceilings; the setting was unimaginably romantic.

41

I could easily have floated there all evening, wandering from bath to bath, soaking in the gentle waters, luxuriating in quiet candlelight. After an hour or so a spa attendant came to fetch me, though. It was time for chocotherapy.

She led me, dripping, to a dimly lit room dominated by a large marble-slab table and indicated that I was to hoist myself up onto the slab. There was no chocolate in sight, but I knew it was nearby. I could smell it: big and rich and sweet. My masseuse entered and introduced herself. "*Hola*. I'm Sandra." She balanced a large bowl of chocolate sauce on the palm of one hand. "Please lie down."

I felt a bit like a corpse, laid out on that marble slab, or maybe like a mummy. But my skin came alive as Sandra smoothed chocolate onto every inch, beginning at my toes and working her way slowly up to my neck. Then she went down to my toes, covering every inch again, just to be sure she hadn't missed any spots.

What exactly was it that covered my body? New World chocolate, thin and bitter? Or the chocolate of chocolate-and-churros, rich and sweet? I wanted to taste it in the worst way. Somehow that didn't seem appropriate, though. I wasn't familiar with the etiquette for a chocolate massage, so I determined to work out the best course of action in a silent conversation with myself:

"You *can't* lick it off."

"But I really want to. I want to taste it."

"Sandra is still rubbing it on; it would be an insult to her work to lick it off."

"I have to taste it. It's research."

"That would be unhygienic."

"I just soaked in the baths. I'm super clean."

"But you would look *so* stupid, licking yourself like a cat."

"And it would taste so good."

"Maybe it wouldn't. How do you know what's in it? Maybe they didn't want to waste sugar in a concoction that no one would ever taste, and it's just bitter chocolate powder and water."

No one would ever taste? All that chocolate—it seemed such a shame! Surely I was not the first person—nor would I be the last— who longed to lick the stuff. I imagined rows of naked ladies, a mahogany-colored sisterhood, covered with chocolate and sitting like cats, licking themselves clean. I liked the idea.

"It's sticky, so there has to be sugar in it," I persisted. "Besides, that's why I have to taste it, to find out for sure."

"What body part would you lick?"

It was then that I realized I'd missed my chance, because Sandra began to swathe me in clear plastic wrap, beginning at my feet and quickly moving all the way up to my shoulders. I felt like a gigantic chocolate Easter bunny, neatly wrapped in cellophane and waiting for the big day—Easter Sunday, coming soon—when some lucky child would pluck me from my nest in a small plastic basket, rip through the see-through wrapping and bite off an ear.

Sandra interrupted my reverie. "I'll leave you here to relax for awhile, OK?"

My arms were trapped at my sides, and things were heating up fast, probably because of the airtight plastic wrap. It wasn't exactly a relaxing situation, but I was ready to be alone. Maybe I could lift my neck up as soon as Sandra left and reach an unwrapped part of my chest with my tongue.

"OK," I said. "Thanks, Sandra."

It would not be unfair to say I was obsessed. Twenty minutes later I was still considering the possibility of licking off the chocolate when Sandra returned. Why, exactly, had I thought anything other than eating was an appropriate use of the tantalizing substance?

"So Sandra," I began. "Is all this chocolate supposed to make my skin soft?"

"*Si*," she replied. "Soft and hydrated." Sandra pronounced it EE-drä-ted. She unwrapped me efficiently and had expertly hosed all the chocolate off my body in a matter of seconds. It slid across my shoulders. It slipped down my back and belly and legs. I watched as it ran across the floor and circled into a drain. All that deliciousness—down the drain so quickly.

"Next is your sugar scrub."

A sugar scrub? After a chocolate massage? The brochure hadn't mentioned this, but what could be more perfect? I relaxed as Sandra scrubbed me down with granules of sugar suspended in a light oil. My skin sparkled like a sugar cookie, glinting in the candlelight.

And I had learned my lesson: This time I would take advantage of any opportunity to sneak a taste. As soon as Sandra turned her head I surreptitiously licked my shoulder ... and got an awful mouthful of argan oil and gigantic, crunchy sugar crystals. Bleeech! There was nowhere to spit; I had to swallow it.

As Sandra hosed me off once again, I contemplated my newly soft and hydrated skin. It had been cloaked in chocolate, dark and earthy, and then reborn, sparkling with light in an unusual—but not inappropriate—celebration of Easter Week. And although my confectionary escapade had come to a close, I still felt delicious.

Cream of Sunshine

Saffron Entranced

Antoinette Constable

We may live without
poetry, music and art;
We may live without
conscience and may live
Without heart;
We may live without
Friends;
We may live without books;
But civilized man
cannot live
without cooks.

—Owen Meredith

My grandmother, Leah Gornick, had an Andalusian cook named Honoria at her pink mansion, Tresvignes, in the south of France. The year was 1945. We, grandmother Leah and her grandchildren, hardly interacted with Honoria. She was thin, had sunken but blazing eyes and spoke little. She came from a village north of Seville whose name was unpronounceable to us. She belonged in the kitchen, a space off limits to the children.

I was a child, to be seen but not heard, and didn't dare to ask why Honoria, rarely seen, was always unsmiling. I once overheard one of the uncles, Oncle André, I think it was, describing her as taciturn. Taciturn? It sounded dreadful, sufficient reason to avoid her.

When Grand-Maman lived in her large apartment in Paris, with beautifully patterned rugs, different sets of china, pink and green jade objects in the salon, we often went to visit. In those days, our grandmother unfailingly provided refined, excellent meals, beautifully presented to the many guests sitting at her large table. They were served oysters, quail, sturgeon, or beef stroganoff, duck à l'orange, lobster-stuffed artichoke hearts, garden peas in poached lettuce nests and desserts like meringue cake layers filled with Mandarin cream, chocolate mousse and filbert custard.

At least, that was the case until the restrictions imposed by the war—World War II, that is. Then our grandmother's lunches and dinners became a thing of the past. We no longer visited. Grand-Maman went into hiding around St. Etienne and in Lyon.

Grand-Maman, you see, was Jewish, of German, American and English ancestry. For her own safety, she had to leave Paris first, then—after her husband died—retreat to her southern property, using a false name.

She, whose cook came to her each morning to plan delectable meals, who had never set foot in the kitchen, had to learn to wait in long lines for bread and margarine-gray pasta, had to shell lima beans, sift lentils to remove bits of pebbles, scrape carrots, peel potatoes, boil water and make soup.

We, too, living in a suburb of Paris, were in dire straits. We had no way of contacting Grand-Maman, but we occasionally received a postcard with no return address, simply signed, "Bonnie."

After the war, we returned to Tresvignes above Cannes, supplying our own sheets and towels, since Grand-Maman's linen had been pillaged by Spanish and German occupiers, together with her Sèvres dishes, books dedicated to her and our grandfather, a rare stamp collection, antique furniture, gold coins, statues and paintings. Throughout the war, Honoria remained at Tresvignes, forced to work without pay for the enemy,

Food restrictions long remained in order. To feed several adults and a gaggle of children come for the summer was difficult. I remember a puree of eggplant, gray and watery, often served at dinner. At least, being close to the Mediterranean, Honoria sometimes bought us fish. Accompanied by chopped onions and turnips, the dish was no treat. Pasta with tomato sauce was better, but the meals didn't appeal.

Grand-Maman ate little, ashamed, I'm sure, to offer us gratins without cheese, dusted instead with bread crumbs, or corn on the cob, considered unfit for human consumption, good enough for cattle at best.

Once, however, the clockwork appearance of vaguely palatable dishes stopped and for a moment we all returned to the past to a merely taciturn rather than brooding Honoria, and a table graced with fine dishes.

On that day, instead of melon, peaches, grapes or figs that figured at the end of our meals, a fabulous dessert was passed around the table. The grown-ups, who often argued vigorously, interrupting each other, fell silent one after the other, as did the cousins, each savoring the content of little pots with round handles the size of garden peas.

A pleasurable peace filled us as we quietly concentrated on retrieving every last smear of this magnificent dessert I christened "Cream of Sunshine." It tasted a tiny bit smoky but smooth and sweet on the tongue with a healthy egg-yellow color and a smell rather like wisteria, only better, or some a rare perfume.

When the conversation started again, smiling aunts and uncles nodded, oohed and aahed as they recalled what they knew about saffron.

Cleopatra, our grumpiest aunt divulged deprecatingly, used saffron to flavor her bath. Nero ordered the spice spread on the streets of Rome before his passage. Pirates of the Mediterranean ignored gold bullion, preferring to pilfer invaluable saffron.

Another aunt revealed that saffron was really the styles and stigmas, or "threads," of a crocus flower. It improved cerebral function and soothed teething in infants.

An uncle declared that it was often used to flavor rice, poultry, tea, coffee and even wine. Under King Henry VIII, saffron was so valued that any detected additive was punishable by imprisonment or even death. Such an outrageous statement! We only pretended to shudder.

We learned that saffron had been used to treat many conditions, from melancholia to wounds and drunkenness. It also contributed to ointments, perfumes and mascara. It was mentioned In the *Song of Solomon*, to describe the lips of the beloved. We, the children, giggled.

Information kept pouring out, with everyone nodding in approval. My cousins and I asked whether we could get some. We were told that saffron had been brought to Spain by the Moors and cultivated in England, France, Greece and Persia, to name only a few countries. What we really wanted to know was whether there was a chance of seconds. That was when one of the aunties stood and announced, "Viva Honoria!" plunking herself down again. Everyone applauded.

Invisible inside her kitchen, mysterious Honoria with a magic wooden spoon and few ingredients had managed to enchant us, delight us and pacify us with this creation in a way no other dessert ever had.

Recipes for good paella with saffron abound. I will not bore you with one more. Instead, here is the fabulous no-cooking, no fuss, delectably flavored dessert Honoria made us.

Cream of Sunshine
(to serve 6)

1 large pot of plain yogurt, preferably Greek
2 tbsp light brown sugar, sweetener or honey
A pinch of saffron threads
¾ cup toasted pistachios
Optional: a ripe mango, peeled and diced small,
    stirred in before serving.

Two days before serving, mix yogurt and sweetener together. Keep refrigerated. The next day, stir again, noticing how the saffron colors the yogurt a vibrant gold color. Mix till smooth. Adjust for sweetness before filling individual dessert cups. Top with pistachios before serving to preserve crunch. Try this divine mixture accompanied by thin ginger cookies. Then, share your reactions with us, please!

Scary Jesus

Scary Jesus

Daphne Beyers

It was a cool night in early spring. Holy Week, when crowds of worshippers gather in the streets of Seville, was a week away. I thought I was safe. My friends and I set out after dark to walk to a restaurant. By day Seville's narrow cobblestone streets fill with pedestrians and mopeds zipping past. By night, these same lonely alleys revert to their medieval origins.

I wasn't quite sure where we were going as I blithely followed my companions down the twisting streets. My footsteps tapped across the cobblestones and my mind drifted. I felt a bit addled from jet lag, that most modern of afflictions. We merged onto Calle Luchana, a broader avenue with shops shuttered against the shadowy eve. Drums beating a slow rhythm sounded from the other end of the lane. I froze in my tracks.

A large crowd filled the street, parading slowly toward us as if in a funeral procession. The men at the head of the crowd wore long white robes. Conical white hats towered above their heads and covered their faces in white cloth, the eye holes cut out. They like looked they belonged to the Ku Klux Klan.

Solemn horns accompanied the slow beat of the drums. Behind the crowd, a bier laboriously rounded the corner, carried aloft by invisible hands. A man stood on the bier, high above the heads of the crowd, dressed in a purple robe. His hands were tied in front of him and a noose hung around his neck. This wasn't a funeral procession. This was a lynching.

The condemned man wobbled stiffly on his moving perch. With a shock I discovered this wasn't a man at all but a realistic-looking mannequin. With an even deeper shock, I realized the mannequin was supposed to be Jesus, the Christ of Christianity. Not the shepherd Jesus who rescued stray lambs, nor the miracle-working Jesus who healed the sick, nor the socially minded Jesus who gave alms to the poor. Nope. This was the condemned criminal Jesus, brutally killed in front of the mob all those centuries ago. This was Scary Jesus.

Maybe if I'd been raised Catholic I would have understood the meaning behind the horror and been more at ease with the spectacle. I'd been to church enough in my youth to learn that Jesus's death was supposed to be a good thing, a necessary step toward mass forgiveness and man's ultimate spiritual growth, but seriously? Nobody really believes that, do they? If they did, Judas's betrayal of Jesus to the temple authorities would have been all part of God's Plan. Judas would be a saint. There was a small cult in the Middle Ages that tried to worship Judas as a saint following this same logic. The Medieval Church burned them all at the stake. And there was Dante; he put Judas in the lowest pit of hell, perpetually chewed by a frozen Lucifer. So why were these people celebrating Jesus's betrayal and execution?

I rejoined my friends, and we picked up our pace. They were eager to get to the restaurant. I was eager to outrun Scary Jesus and the growing mob that surrounded him—religious procession or not.

I don't remember what I ate. I was just glad to be inside a well-lit room surrounded by the trappings of modern civilization. No more medieval stuff for me. I relaxed. I enjoyed the meal and the convivial conversations with my mates. I let down my guard ... and Scary Jesus found me. At first I wasn't sure what I was hearing. It sounded like a distant rumble. Then the din shaped into a rhythmic drumming. I was on the second floor, which should have protected me from whatever was coming my way, but the waiters, mistaking my growing agitation for religious fervor, opened the balcony doors.

Scary Jesus had arrived. The mob paraded below me, larger than before. They carried the bier above their heads. This put Scary Jesus at exactly eye level to where I stood gripping the balcony's guardrail with white knuckles. Worse yet, the exhausted bier carriers stopped to take a break right there in the narrow passageway just outside the restaurant, leaving me to stare directly into Scary Jesus's eyes. This was not a pretty sight. Jesus's face was strained and gaunt and painted with blood dripping down his cheeks. By now the crowd had swelled to hundreds of people. Looking down on the masses milling about below, I imagined torches and pitchforks and a mob braying for blood.

New carriers were found to replace their worn companions. When the bier finally moved on, I breathed a shaky sigh of relief. I don't begrudge Catholics their ceremonies. I'm happy for people who find something to believe in, something that gives them hope in a world torn by violence and senseless cruelty. The days of the Spanish Inquisition are long over. But history does have a way of repeating itself and turning the world retrograde for a time. On that balcony I felt as if I were looking into the past, not the present, back to a time when people were burned in the name of a man who, ironically, preached love and forgiveness.

We finished our dinner, a fine meal laced with much wine. On the way back to our hotel, we ran into the procession once more. I was too new to the twisting alleyways to figure out a route around the procession and so were my other companions, so we were forced to follow behind the troupe. It was close to midnight by then. The procession had been marching for hours, and the mood of the crowd had shifted, the waning gravitas replaced by jubilation and high spirits. Perhaps it was the wine. People on balconies overlooking the street danced and waved at the crowd. The drums beat more heartily, and the horns played happier tunes. The whole city, it seemed, was celebrating.

By then I had actually gotten used to seeing Scary Jesus. Maybe that was the real trick. If you grew up seeing Scary Jesus everywhere, maybe he wasn't so scary anymore. The joyous crowd had turned from a medieval mob into a party reminiscent of Fat Tuesday.

From what I understand, Holy Week dedicates six days to Jesus's torture and death. Then on the last day comes the resurrection part. Jesus defeats death and everyone celebrates. The Spanish, in particular, love this sort of thing. It is part of their national psyche. Spanish poets talk about the joy inside death. Federico García Lorca famously said, "In Spain the dead are more alive than the dead of any country in the world."

I have no idea what that means, but somehow it perfectly sums up the Spanish outlook on life for me. It seems these men and women live in a present rooted in the traditions of the past, something most Americans find far too complicated and fail to understand.

At last we came to where we'd begun our walk. I slipped away from the crowd. The Spanish stay up late, especially on a Saturday night, and the streets still thronged with revelers. The hotel, however, was quiet. On the whole, I was glad to have been given a small glimpse into Holy Week. I was sure I could never endure an entire week of solemn processions, but for one night I saw into the heart of Spanish culture, past, present, and future.

The Madonna

SEVILLE'S MOST HOLY WEEK

Anne Sigmon

I remember that night in Seville as a whirling blur of light, color, music and raw emotion. It was mid-March, 2016. Yellow candles flickered on a raised carpet of red roses; the air quivered with the scent of incense and orange blossoms; my ears rang with the hypnotic dirge of drums and the wail of trumpets in the minor key of grief. Onlookers crammed onto narrow streets, arms lifted, angling cameras and cellphones to capture the image of Christ, robed in midnight blue, standing high above them on a flower-bedecked float. His hands were tied, a crown of thorns shoved low on his brow, his head tilted, mouth open as if to say, "I forgive."

The exuberant participants who ushered the float through winding streets that night—men, women, teens, and tots, un-costumed, most wearing jeans and windbreakers—melded with the spectators in one excited crush of followers.

Before I realized it, I was one of them.

The procession took me by surprise. I never expected to find myself caught up in a throng of celebrants that night. It was Saturday, a full week before Palm Sunday, the official start of *Semana Santa*—Holy Week. I'd just finished dinner with several friends at a restaurant on Serpientes Street near Seville's Cathedral when I heard the rat-a-tat of snare drums and the peal of a trumpet fanfare.

That sound took me back six years, to 2010, when I'd spent Holy Week in Seville with my husband, two among more than a million citizens and visitors who jammed the streets to watch the world's largest Easter celebration: vibrant, colorful, noisy, both solemn and joyous—and all-consuming.

Carefully keeping to the sidelines to respect the religious tenor of the week, we'd observed *Semana Santa's* annual eight-day extravaganza of meticulously planned processions—as many as ten a day—wind through the city's ancient serpentine streets. Each day, legions of churchmen and women called *Nazarenos*—members of Seville's fifty-six Catholic lay brotherhoods—donned robes and hoods and carried four-foot candles as they escorted priceless wooden floats called *pasos* through the city's streets from their parish churches to the Cathedral and back. For some, it was a journey of twelve hours or more. The floats, resplendent with silver and gold fittings, bore much-venerated life-sized, carved wooden images of Christ and the Virgin Mary, some more than 400 years old. Before each *paso*, elegantly costumed marching bands strode in practiced military precision.

Six years ago, though I'd been dazzled by the pageantry, I'd wondered what lay at its core: What compels *Sevillianos* to repeat the madness year after year? What, in an increasingly secular western world, drives an entire city to spend untold millions of dollars, hours, sweat, and tears on a spectacle of religious fervor?

I turned to Pilar Rubio, resident of Seville and new friend, for some insight. In her thirties, with glasses and long, dark hair that swings when she's animated, Pilar is both an expert and a participant in Seville's Holy Week. "The *Semana Santa* celebration is very personal," she told me. Even though Pilar doesn't consider herself particularly religious, she's a member of two of Seville's brotherhoods, one in her neighborhood church, and—closest to her heart—one in the neighborhood where she grew up and where her grandfather and father were both members. She often marches as a barefoot, penitent *Nazareno*.

To Pilar, *Semana Santa* captures a visceral sense of Christianity. "There's a feeling of belonging when you participate in the Holy Week processions—to be part of a tradition that's been going on for four hundred years. Besides, even if you're not from our tradition, it's almost impossible not to be caught up in it."

She's right about that, I thought, remembering one special day from 2010. As the *paso* bearing the virgin passed us on a narrow street, the woman beside me—who'd been chatting amiably a few moments before—crossed herself, threw a kiss, and began to cry. When the float stopped, a hush fell over the crowd. From a balcony above, a high soprano voice in operatic tone sang a piercing *saeta*—song of lamentation—as white candles flickered over the Virgin's radiant but tragic face.

But there was also an ebullient, family atmosphere that sometimes felt more like a county fair than church. Boys with dark ringlets danced in the street, high on soda and excitement. Little girls with balloons tied to their wrists rode their father's shoulders to get a better view. During breaks, children buzzed around the *Nazarenos,* begging them for melted candle wax. It was odd to see these spectral, hooded figures—many walking barefoot in penance—turn and silently tilt their long candles downward to the eager kids, who collected the pooling wax, then molded it into bright-colored balls of mischief.

Historian Elizabeth Nash once described *Semana Santa* as "an annual explosion of emotion that is part devotion, part fiesta." It sure seemed that way to me.

This year, I was alone, unfettered and curious. This night's unexpected procession might offer a chance to learn more. Straining to hear the music from the approaching band, I shivered with the same tinge of the excitement I'd felt six years ago. Leaving my dinner companions, I wandered out into the street to watch.

I noticed right away that this procession was different from any I had seen on my first visit. The only *paso* was a simple one: Christ

61

walking on a ground of roses, no silver or gold to enrich the float, no Virgin *paso*, no lavishly robed and hooded attendants—just a few altar boys dressed in white cassocks who carried crosses in front of the *paso*. Five high-school girls, dressed in school jumpers, hoisted candles and wooden crosses. Band members sported blue and gray sweaters that didn't quite match. They all mingled on the sidelines and in the street with young people dressed mostly in blue-gray jeans and jackets. Onlookers merged with marchers, everyone taking cell-phone photos.

Costaleros—the beefy men who carry the *pasos*—in white T-shirts and beige headgear, moved in and out of the procession, in shifts. At the breaks, they stepped away to refresh themselves with yellow cones of chips and plastic cups of beer supplied by their friends on the sidelines. When it was time to go again, the foreman (called a *capataz)* whispered a "get-ready" signal to thirty *costaleros,* who were hidden under the heavy float behind a red velvet skirt. Then he hammered— *smack*—on the edge of the float. The men growled an audible *hup.* The more than 2,000-pound *paso* jumped to attention, rose from the ground like Lazarus, and began to waltz slowly down the street to adoring applause.

The crowd was casual and animated. Many of them wore the same gray-blue as the marchers—parishioners and family members, I guessed. One little girl, barely old enough to walk, stood out, dressed all in pink—a frilly dress, matching tights and a pink satin bow in her hair. She waved at me, and I waved back.

I walked along the sidewalk following the band. Many of the musicians were young, perhaps high school and college age. I clapped in time as a particularly animated trumpeter filed past me. Her ponytail danced with the rhythm of the music as she marched.

Gradually, the mood changed. The dirge pace of the snare drums lulled me into a trance. Dum, dum, dum-te-de-dum. The smell of burning candles and incense wafted from the float. As I watched and listened to the drums, I felt increasingly spellbound.

The night was dark and chilly. Just in front of me, two parishioners in wheelchairs rolled directly behind the Christ float. One—a woman —suffered from a humped back, short legs and a foreshortened body. She rode in the kind of specialized chair I suspected she never left. Wearing a rumpled raincoat and shearling slippers, she propelled herself along using her wheelchair's electric controls. But in what I imagined was an effort to dress up for the occasion, her hands were freshly manicured with blood-red nails. I smiled at her. Then she waved her hand, motioning for to me to come walk beside her. We moved in silence to the cadence of the drums.

A mother pushed a pram with a swaddled infant inside. Then I noticed a little boy of about four, dressed in jeans and a gray sweater, squeezing his mother's hand. As the band played, they walked together close alongside the *paso*. When the procession halted, the *paso* fluttered down onto the pavement. Mother and son stopped. The red drape parted just a bit, and the boy burrowed his left hand under the curtain, holding onto his dad, one of the invisible *costaleros*. All I saw of the father were jean legs and tennis shoes the color of his tiny son's sweater.

People at sidewalk cafés joined in the celebration as the *paso* marched by. Young people on the sidelines sipped beer and smoked cigarettes, putting on their best cool. *They aren't participating this year,* I thought, *but they are here. Semana Santa* is part of the fabric of their lives. Before long, they will be marching in the procession with their babes in strollers. They'll bring their children to celebrate Seville's holiest week, just as their parents brought them.

Our procession left the cobblestone streets of the old town and headed across asphalt streets into the working-class neighborhood of San Bernardo, known as the home of arms factories, firemen and famous bullfighters. It was late; I had no idea where we were headed, and I didn't care. I surrendered to the energy around me and kept walking, no longer an observer, now subsumed in the moment. Above us, the San Bernardo Bridge—sometimes called the Bridge of the Firefighters—was jammed with onlookers whistling and clapping as we made our way slowly past. The image of the Christ, standing tall on the uplifted *paso,* reached almost to the height of the spectators on the bridge. They clapped and hooted, cheering as if he were a live rock star. Some reached out as though to touch him as the float passed by.

I was surprised when the *paso* stopped and, in a series of jerky motions, the *costaleros* turned it perpendicular to the street and headed into the open bay of a firehouse. Inside, the fire brigade stood erect and reverent, their hands clasped behind their backs. The *paso* paused, as though Christ were blessing the firefighters. Then Jesus on his floating altar backed up and headed down the street.

My spine tingled. The crowd roared louder and louder, cheering for the fate of the Lord. More than a thousand people were gathered on the bridge, but soon, all I could hear were the drums. Dum-te-de-dum.

After we left the firehouse, the crowd moved on as one with me still in the middle, stepping in slow time to the beating of the *snares.* The reality of marching block after block faded into reverie, then trance. Everything I'd ever felt, or believed, or thought I knew, swirled in an emotion I couldn't explain. I felt somehow outside myself, not conscious of time or place.

The joys and recent sorrows of my life welled up in that instant. Everything I'd ever hoped for or regretted, every soul I'd lost, returned to me in the surge of Christ's passion and—even if just for a moment—I believed. I marched on through the veil of incense to the dirge of pounding drums, just another penitent seeking salvation.

Antonio Machado

NOTES ON SPANISH POETRY
Thanasis Maskaleris

The best way to appreciate, to be moved, by the poetry of Andalusia is to connect with—to experience—the life of Andalusia. The people of Andalusia are intoxicated by life, and the poetry of Andalusian poets captures and expresses that intoxication—it dances the flamenco.

I have been "living" with Spanish poetry for more than fifty years, since my first journey into Spain. My connection with it has intensified with my exposure to the flamenco/*cante jondo* sounds and García Lorca's "Duende." The foreign reader needs to attune herself-himself to the poetry by reading aloud—best by hearing the original Spanish—to experience the sound, the rhythms of the poems.

Antonio Machado

Caminante son tu huellas
Walker, it is only your footprints
that are the road, nothing more.
Wayfarer, there is no road;
the road is made by walking.

Walking makes the road,
and when looking back,
the track is seen that will never
be the path again.
Walker, there is no road,
Only wake-trails in the sea.

Bueno es saber que los vasos
The good thing is we know
that glasses are for drinking;
the bad thing is we don't know
what our thirst is for ...

La Primavera ha venido
Spring has come;
No one knows how it was done ...

El ojo que ves ...
The eye you see is not an eye
because you see it;
It's an eye because it sees you ...

Federico García Lorca

La Guitarra

The lament of the guitar begins.
The goblets of dawn are smashed.
The weeping of the guitar begins.
Useless to attempt to silence it.
Impossible to silence it.
It weeps monotonously as water weeps,
as the wind weeps over snowfields.
Impossible to silence it.
It cries for distant things—
scalding southern sands yearning for white camellias.
It mourns the arrow without target,
the evening without morning
and the first dead bird on the branch.
Oh, guitar! Heart mortally wounded by five swords.

—Translations by Thanasis Maskaleris

Jesús del Gran Poder in Seville

EASTER RISING:
Una Reconversión Personal

MJ Pramik

I. Procession

Through the narrow street there come
strange unicorns.
From what field,
from what mythological forest?
Circling closer,
They look like astronomers.
Fantastic Merlins
And the condemned Christ
Enchanted Durandarte,
Frenzied Orlando.

—From *Procession** by Federíco García Lorca

As a recovering Catholic, I instinctively joke with strangers and friends alike when they introduce religion into a conversation. Intellectual deduction, scientific training and a partiality to Bill Maher's *Religulous* (a gift from my three pagan-baby children) has led me to beeline toward a fierce agnosticism, particularly since the deaths of my staunchly devout parents a decade ago. True Polish Roman Catholics to the end, they no longer hover on the phone, petitioning me for continued church attendance or the baptism of their grandchildren, neither at Christmastime with its sweet hymns, nor at Easter with its sober fare. I came of age during Vatican II, living through the rebellion of priests and nuns at my Jesuit college. We *all* converted the bread and wine into Jesus's body and blood. The clergy scandals of the past two decades put the finishing touch on any lingering Catholic sentiment in my mind. And my heart.

Nonetheless, a recent stroll through the narrow streets of Seville on a cool Saturday night in March—the week before the festivities of *Semana Santa*—revealed several deep-seated passages hidden in my psyche. Federico García Lorca's poem *Procession* exquisitely conveys the magic I experienced that evening while ambling down Calle Placentines.

In hindsight, my "reconversion" had begun in Madrid a few days earlier. I'd stopped in Spain's capital city for three brief hours while waiting for the afternoon train to Seville. When one has only three hours to spend in Madrid, one visits the Museo del Prado, home to vast collections of works by Goya, El Greco, and Diego Rodríguez de Silva y Velázquez. Velázquez's work flows through ten galleries, overpowering an entire wing. After a short taxi hop from the Atocha Station, my expat friend Maryly and I alighted at the museum stairs. She, ecstatic over the current exhibit of French Neoclassical painter Ingres, bolted down one of the halls in search of his 1862 masterpiece *The Turkish Bath*.

As for me, I savored simply standing there, in the entrance of the Prado, in Spain, on a cold, sunny day in March. I began to wander the galleries, mesmerized by all paintings Velázquez. Floating from room to room, I found his religious paintings created an otherworldly atmosphere. The subjects—king, dwarf, pope, child, Jesus of Nazareth —their shared essence lifted me. Remnants of the mental fog of jet lag? No: the painter's insight, his ability to convey hu-manity's universal grace as the central mystery of the Catholic faith. *Christ Crucified*, dating from 1632, seemed almost contemporary, with Christ's shaggy hair draping over his right eye and cheek, his strained physique so beautiful in death. On that canvas, I beheld Velázquez's belief that Jesus was dignified and beautiful even when bloodied and broken. Intermingled with his renderings of dwarfs, kings and princesses, the Christ crucified entranced.

From the Museo I rushed back to my train and was whisked to Seville's Santa Justa station, where some friends convinced me an immediate visit to the Cathedral of Saint Mary of the See was in order. Even with its multitude of altars for Spain's current royalty and assorted saints, the Cathedral seemed empty. None of the *pasos*, the enormous, elaborate processional floats made for the following week's *Semana Santa* ceremonies, had yet appeared in the open expanse.

On our way to dinner that evening, our group met with a small procession transporting the most forlorn Christ statue I've ever seen. In purple robe, head crowned with thorns, bound hands crossed in front of his robe's folds, the figure tottered five feet above my head on the *paso*. The crowd of several hundred, thick and unhurried, followed the drum-and-trumpet band. Youths marched and played their brass, the tuba rocking large behind the statue, with solemn beat and surging horns.

The *paso* is moved by porters, or *costaleros*, hidden under a long skirt. These *costaleros* line up four and five across, in five- or six-line rows under the litter. A *capataz*, or "head man," shouts into the front section of the *paso*. The *costaleros* cannot pick up or set down the *paso* until the *llamado*, or crier, signals. These men moved in coordinated steps; the musicians, fervent and triumphant, creating a sense that this Jesus was floating on his own power.

Winding our way homewards after dinner, we yet again came across the same *paso* as it coiled its way through the streets. Without intention, I fell into step as the *paso* once more snaked past me, roping me into its spell. The *costaleros* peeked out from under the float's skirt, smiled and winked at me in their white tank tops, multicolored bandanas wrapped around their dark hair.

Percussion thrumming, brass instruments intensifying ... I walked with a family—mother, five-year-old daughter, grandmother and grandfather (head of the tribe)—behind the weeping Jesus carried by the younger woman's husband and brother among the forty hidden men under the dais. The procession plodded through Seville's narrow alleyways, some so tight only a small car could squeeze through. When the *paso* turned the corner, it did so in clipped, angular movements, the *costaleros* coordinating their footwork while hoisting the two-thousand-pound structure, heeding the rhythm of the drums. Tears in my throat, incense smoke clouding my eyes, I marched with this *paso* until well past midnight as we wended our way through dimly lit streets.

II. *Paso*
Virgin with glittering crinoline skirts,
virgin of solitude,
In your boat of lights
you sail
with the high tide
of the city,
among gypsy songs
and crystal stars.

Virgin with glittering crinoline skirts,
you float
on the river of the street—
to the sea!

—From *Procession** by Federico García Lorca

Through my travel group's excellent guide, Estela Gonzalez, I met Sara Santacana Roales, an energetic millennial from the working-class Triana sector of Seville. I spent an evening with Sara discussing Triana, where *Semana Santa* traditions differ from the practices of the city center, and we immediately bonded over our parallel family histories. Her relatives were *gitanos,* the Spanish Romani persecuted by non-Roma Spaniards for hundreds of years. My Polish ancestors had suffered similar oppression in their native land, first under German and Prussian rulers, then during the ethnic cleansing of World War II and subsequent Polish anti-religious campaigns. Throughout these hardships, both of our families had held fast to their Roman Catholic faith. In discussing the persecution of my forebears, the visceral connection to my spiritual roots was reignited. Sara, too, considered herself a non-practicing Catholic, but through discussion, the strength of our belief in our common divine origin intensified.

Sara met me at the Iglesia San Salvador in central Seville at twilight the evening after our heart-to-heart. The hollow sound of hammers readying the *pasos* for Holy Week echoed as night approached. Walking among them, we gazed up at the church's central effigy of Christ: Juan de Mesa's *Brotherhood of Love.* The statue was crafted in 1618 in honor of the incarcerated prisoners of Spain, in the hopes of imparting Christ's love to all penitents.

II. Saeta (Gypsy processional song)
The swarthy Christ
transforms
from the lily of Judea
to the carnation of Spain.
Look where he's coming from!
From Spain,
The sky, clean and dark,
The earth scorched,
And ditches where
Water runs very slowly.
Swarthy Christ,
His locks of hair burned,
His cheekbones protruding
And his pupils white.
Look where he's going!

—From *Procession* * by Federico García Lorca

Throughout her childhood, Sara, her family and grandparents all came together to share Holy Week in the city, just as my Polish family had done in rural Maynard, Ohio. Her clan attended church, prayed, genuflected as the Christ figures were carried through the streets, but as the more pious relatives passed away and twenty-first-century life took over, Sara had drifted into the same skeptical limbo in which I currently found myself. When I asked how she felt about Holy Week this year, Sara said she'd avoid brooding over the ideologies of the Catholic Church and instead allow herself to experience the overwhelming emotions of the ceremonies by staying in the present. This essence of emotion surging from the pit of our stomachs or the ache in our chests is precisely what the *pasos*, the effigies, the theater, the music of *Semana Santa* hurl out into the world. I suddenly realized I'd already felt this power—dare I say, this *duende*—myself as I marched with the *paso* on my first night in Seville, following the loving, forlorn Jesus through the streets.

I prepared for my return to California in a state of serenity. As the drums pounded on the *Semana Santa* videos, Sara graciously continued to email for my edification. I heard her voice in my head: "I was always taught that in dying, you rise again. We celebrate the God of Love amidst suffering, the endless baptism of freshly created days."

Having returned from Seville on Palm Sunday, I spent *Semana Santa* in San Francisco enveloped in frigid fog, amid misty mornings hiding the lemon sun that rushes into the sky. I could feel the *paso* of the children with Jesus's triumphal entry into Jerusalem on that day. This year, when Good Friday arrived, I paid attention. On Holy Saturday a quietude settled in, followed by the tranquility of Easter Sunday. Over the last decade, I'd normally spent the day hiking into the Marin hills and dining with nearby family friends.

This year, a new passion arose, and I chose to remain alone with my sentiments, alone with the power of *duende*. I rediscovered that *alegría*, that joy. Then, reflecting on the passion of Lorca's words and the immediacy of the mysteries surrounding me, I wrote:

> *On Easter, the gingko awoke.*
> *It sprouted—overnight it seems—*
> *Joyous green tiny gingko leaves,*
> *Those fan-shaped fingers created*
> *In another millennium eons*
> *Ago when the earth convulsed*
> *Without the concept of time*
> *On a lateral, flat plane*
> *To nowhere.*

On Easter, I descended the steps
Of my home boarded off from
The natural world as such
Save for the kitchen ants
Who accompany my morning coffee.
On descending those concrete lavers
The reborn gingko
Greeted me: Awake! Awake!
It shook me in the gentle
Sunday breeze filming about my face.

"Look what I have for you,"
This quiet tree hummed.
An old Easter hymn rose
In my throat,
"All in the early morning gray,
Went holy women on their way
To see the tomb where Jesus lay
Alleluia, alleluia, alleluia,
Alleluia."

Sign marking Susona's home in the Jewish Quarter

A JEWISH QUARTER WITHOUT JEWS

Donna Hemmila

For generations, my family's Jewish roots lay hidden. I grew up Catholic, attending mass six days a week with my parochial school classmates, confessing my sins, collecting money for the *pagan babies*, and amassing a stack of holy cards depicting the A-list saints and martyrs. My Uncle Tommy's idea of entertainment on road trips was to pray along with the radio's *Rosary Hour*. I was, indeed, 100 percent Catholic.

Or so I thought.

Then last year, my Aunt Nancy, my mother's sister, received a mail-in DNA test as a gift. The results revealed that my ancestors hailed from Eastern Europe. I knew that. My grandparents were Polish and Croatian. What I didn't know about was the 3 percent Ashkenazi Jew buried deep in our family's DNA.

Initial reaction from various family members has ranged from "I knew it!" to a skeptical "Three percent? That's within the statistical margin of error, isn't it?" For myself, I welcomed this tiny slice of Jewishness to the mix of me with enthusiasm. "Visit Seville's Jewish Quarter" promptly moved to the top of my Andalusia must-see list.

A month later, on a sun-drenched Sunday morning, I set out on a walking tour of Seville's Juderia, eager to feed my tiny, withered Jewish roots.

Since the city had once sheltered one of the largest and most prosperous Jewish populations in Spain, I anticipated finding a still-thriving Jewish neighborhood similar to the Marais. On my way to Spain, I had visited that traditionally Jewish neighborhood in Paris and found a lively community with synagogues, bookstores, kosher restaurants, charcuteries and bakeries. Surely I'd experience the same in Seville.

But I'd soon discover that—like my own Jewish ancestry—Seville's Jewish Quarter has been erased, replaced with a layer of deeply ingrained Christianity. A walk through the quarter's narrow cobbled streets revealed a history of things that aren't there anymore. The synagogues, the stately homes, the culture, the people themselves are all gone. As with the pains from a phantom limb, I could only sense what used to be and mourn its loss.

At the start of our walking tour, our guide pointed out the easy-to-overlook brass plaques embedded in sidewalks and buildings to designate Jewish sites of historical interest—or rather where those sites used to be.

As we wound our way through a labyrinth of uneven stone streets, rather than discovering tributes to Jewish culture, we found a charming tourist paradise, where shops, cafes and custard-colored houses trimmed in shades of salmon and sunrises line the traffic-free passageways. Overhead, wrought-iron balconies overflow with pots of fire-red and brilliant pink geraniums. The shops at street level sell all the Andalusian souvenirs the heart could desire. I bought a silk fan with a pattern of magenta and orange flowers. Many of the private homes leave their front doors open, revealing tranquil courtyards where fountains trickle and orange trees bloom. But we learned from our guide that the custom of open front doors had sinister, medieval roots. *Conversos*, Jews forced to adopt Christianity to survive, were suspected of practicing their Jewish religion in secret. Laws required them to leave their doors open so the authorities could more conveniently spy on them.

Whenever our group strolled by one of these homes, we all stopped to snap photos and inhale the orange blossom perfume. Unfortunately, the heavenly scented orange trees everywhere in Seville bear an inedible sour fruit destined for jars of British marmalade. Sweetness masking bitter truths—a fitting metaphor for the Jewish Quarter.

As I walked the streets of Seville's Jewish Quarter, its very name raised a quiet resentment in me: Barrio Santa Cruz, the Neighborhood of the Holy Cross, the most sacred of Christian symbols. As if the Jews needed a reminder that they no longer had a right to call these streets home.

An iron cross sits in the center of Plaza Santa Cruz, once the site of the barrio's main synagogue. A Catholic church replaced it after a fourteenth-century pogrom. In a twist of fate, Napoleon's troops destroyed the church five centuries later. The nearby Santa María la Blanca and San Bartolemé churches, as well as the Madre de Dios convent, all used to be synagogues. At one time, the city contained twenty-three. Now there are none. How this startling decline came about is a centuries-long story of persecution and resentment.

Some historians speculate that merchant Jews could have arrived in Andalusia as early as the tenth century BCE when the Phoenicians reigned. Other scholars suggest Jews migrated to Spain after the destruction of the temple in Jerusalem in 70 CE. I'm no historian, so I find the variations on the early days of Sephardic, or Spanish, Jews as confusing as Seville's twisty streets. One thing for sure, their lives in Andalusia shifted dangerously between periods of tolerance and vicious persecution.

The Christian Visigoths, who ruled Spain after the decline of Rome, decreed all Jewish religious and cultural practices off limits. Violation of these laws carried a death sentence. This wave of oppression lasted until the Muslim invasion in 711 when al-Andalus was born. The invading Moors blessed Spain with science, scholarship, breath-taking architecture and religious tolerance. On a visit to Seville's famous Alcázar, I saw the Star of David emblazoned in tile and plaster alongside Muslim designs.

After King Ferdinand III liberated Seville from the Moors in 1248, Jews coexisted with their Christian neighbors. Many held prominent positions as scholars, doctors, financiers, poets and artists. One such noteworthy citizen served as treasurer to King Pedro I. Samuel Levi was a trusted court advisor until jealous rivals accused him of embezzling money from the treasury. He was arrested, tortured and executed in 1361.

We passed the site of Samuel Levi's house—or where it used to stand before it was torn down after his murder. Our guide tells us people swarmed the home after his arrest, digging for the embezzled treasure he allegedly buried there. They found none. For me that is a small bright spot among the many stories of grief and hardship.

In the fourteenth century, things started to go south for the Jews in a big way. Hard economic times coupled with the Black Plague sent Spaniards looking for scapegoats. In 1391, spurred on by the preaching of a local archdeacon, the people of Seville stormed the Jewish Quarter setting fires and killing 4,000 Jews. The remaining Jews either fled or were forced to convert.

I'd read books and seen films about pogroms against the Jews. But I had never stood on ground where these horrors actually happened. Stepping on this sacred earth, it felt like a fist gripping my heart.

Life got worse for the Jews with the launching of the Spanish Inquisition, headquartered in a castle across the Guadalquivir River in Seville. Hundreds of Jews were tried and sentenced to death. Today on the same site of their torture, the Museo de Castillo de San Jorge serves as an Inquisition museum.

The final blow came in 1492. King Ferdinand and Queen Isabella completed their *Reconquista* of Spain with the fall of Granada. Soon after, they expelled all Jews from the country. Some fled to Portugal, where a few decades later they were also expelled. Others ended up in Northern European countries, Northern Africa, the Middle East, and eventually the New World.

Today, in a city with a population of more than 700,000, where in the mid-fourteenth century 6,000 to 7,000 Jews lived, there are only about 150, scattered among various neighborhoods outside Barrio Santa Cruz.

The Jewishness of the Jewish Quarter hides in plain sight, but you need to dive deep to discover it. At first glance no one would guess, for example, that a restaurant hides the remnants of a centuries-old *mikveh* where Jewish woman gathered for purifying baths, or that a popular flamenco show is housed in the mansion of a fifteenth-century Jewish family.

A few place names offer clues to the community that once thrived here. A sign for Puerta de la Carne, the Gate of Meat, designates the area where kosher butchers did business. There is Calle Levie and Calle Juderia, and then there is Calle Susona, also known as the Street of Death.

Part legend, part history, Susona's story of intrigue and betrayal rivals the tragedy of *Romeo and Juliet*. This beautiful fifteenth-century young Jewish woman fell in love with a Christian nobleman. One night, she heard her father and his friends plotting against their Christian oppressors. Fearing her beloved would be harmed, Susona ran to warn him. This proved to be a foolish move. Her father and his cohorts were arrested and executed. And the lover dumped her. Accounts of the legend have alternate endings, none of them particularly pleasant. Some versions say she entered a convent. Others say she lived out her days a recluse in her father's home, never leaving the confines of its walls. When Susona died, her will contained instructions to sever her head and place it above the door of her home as a gruesome warning to other young women not to betray their people. Much to my relief, the withered head no longer adorns the building. Instead, a ceramic tile with a picture of a skull marks the spot. No one knows what happened to the head.

The most heartbreaking—and to me inexplicably cruel—reminder of a once glorious Jewish heritage lies in an obscure, dank corner of an underground public parking garage. When our guide led us down the steep stairs to the garage, I thought we were taking a shortcut. Shockingly, as we huddled among the parked cars, we learned that we were standing on a former Jewish graveyard. When the city needed a parking garage, it removed the remains, but left a grave intact. As a tribute? A glass window embedded in the gray, sooty walls of the garage provides a view of a single stone sarcophagus. Claustrophobia closed in on me as I tried to digest yet another too literal example of how well Seville buried its Jewish past. I looked at this grave and wondered who rests there and how they died. I wished my 3 percent of Jewishness harbored a Hebrew prayer for the dead. But I only know Catholic prayers.

The day after our walking tour, I set out on my own to visit the Centro de Interpretacion Juderia de Sevilla. Tucked away in Barrio Santa Cruz, this museum opened in 2012 to honor the city's Jewish heritage. I sought it out to lift the weight our walking tour had dropped on my soul.

After purchasing a ticket from the lone employee present, I entered a back room with a small collection of Jewish artifacts, photographs and documents. A portion of one wall is dedicated to Sephardic women who keep their faith and traditions alive in far-flung corners of the globe. I found a bit of solace in one of the quotes on the wall: "Women are the salt and the yeast without which we would not exist."

I circled the room several times searching for the elusive doorway that would lead to the rest of the museum. There wasn't one. What I could see in this one room is all I would get.

But at least it is here, I thought, *and I'm glad I came.* The kind woman who sold me the ticket offered a map of the quarter with the Jewish sites-that-used-to-be clearly numbered and described in Spanish, English and French. Perhaps the very existence of this tiny center signals Seville's willingness finally to acknowledge its Jewish heritage.

On a grander scale, the Spanish government is making an attempt at atonement. In October 2015, more than 500 years after Spain expelled the Jews, its parliament passed a law offering citizenship to all Jews who can prove their Spanish heritage and have a "link" to Spain. The link can include, among other conditions, proof of having studied Spanish culture or history or the ability to speak Ladino, the dialect once prominent among Sephardic Jews.

There are an estimated 3.5 million Jews who trace their ancestry to Spain. No one knows how many will take the government up on its offer, and if they do, how many will actually return to live in the homeland of their ancestors. I suspect some who will take advantage of this olive branch will view it as a purely symbolic way to reclaim part of their deeply buried heritage. I can relate to that.

The Jews who centuries ago deposited their DNA on my family tree remain a mystery to me. Were they, like the Sephardic Jews, forced to convert? Or did they simply intermarry with Christians out of choice? I'll never know.

What I *do know* is you don't have to be Jewish to appreciate the rich legacy Jews left behind in Seville and to wish for the return of an era when Christians, Muslims and Jews lived in harmony. Even if my 3 percent of Jewish DNA is nothing more than a statistical anomaly, it doesn't matter. I'm proud and grateful for this small, tenuous connection to a people who gave the world so much grace and beauty. Perhaps I have increased my Jewish ancestry a few percentage points by walking in their footsteps in Seville.

Gypsy Guitarist

DUENDE

Gayle McGill

"Why would anyone call a restaurant *Duende*?" I asked my husband setting the menu down on a heavy wooden table at one of Oakland's new eating spots. "Didn't your guitar teacher go on and on about *duende* being some kind of evil, death-soaked force that would subsume your very being should you so much as strum a bar of flamenco music?"

He pulled out his phone and checked with Siri, which told him that *duende* is "an imp or goblin-like creature."

I was still at a loss, and in less then a week I was heading to Seville with a group of travel writers. I wanted to understand and be ready to experience this most Spanish of forces. The programmer in me needed a firm definition, or better yet, a checklist. I did not yet know that an Andalusian child—not a checklist—would be my guide.

Three days later, as I read through my notes on the plane to Seville, *duende* entered the lexicon in 1924 as an elf-imp. Web images showed an array of diminutive misshapen figures almost always wearing a pointed gnome hat. Over time the word morphed into "magical" or "enchanting," as in a magical experience. But it was in 1933 that the word *duende* took a giant leap forward. Federico García Lorca, the esteemed Spanish poet and playwright delivered an astoundingly beautiful lecture in Buenos Aires called *Juego y teoria del duende* (*Play and Theory of the Duende*). I read and re-read the text.

The first point Lorca makes is that although *duende* has every-thing to do with the spirit of authentic art and all can sense it, *duende* itself is inexplicable. Not a good start for a checklist. His next point is that *duende* must welcome the possibility of death. That, according to Lorca, makes Spaniards, specifically Andalusians, extremely good at recognizing this force because they embrace death like no other culture on earth; they become almost alive in death.

Lorca, with the poet in him shining through, instructs that *duende* is dark. It is deep. It is truthful. It is mysterious. It is raw, secret, shuddering. It is the true struggle. It lives on the edge.

On the bright side, Lorca contends that *duende* is rooted in the earth, is completely original and brings new and fresh sensations. *Duende* offers a poetic escape from this world and a communication with the divine through the five senses.

Lastly, any art form, or life, for that matter, has the potential to experience *duende*.

Just three years after delivering this brilliant lecture, Lorca the man who had written "all that has dark sound has *duende*" was ripped from a fellow poet's home and executed by Franco's Nationalists. He was thirty-eight years old.

After Lorca, *duende*—the transformative power of authentic art to move a person—was out and running. All subsequent discussions start by acknowledging Lorca.

Flamenco is most often associated with *duende*. Some see it in the soul of the blues and jazz. Bob Dylan always had it. Leonard Cohen dealt specifically in it, and to find it in the movies I needed to look no farther than Ingmar Bergman.

I shifted in my middle seat, loosened my seatbelt, and read through the last few articles I'd downloaded from the Internet the day before.

One piece focused on the intensity of the physical/emotional response to art. Another stressed the role of the observer as part of the creative act with a kind of feedback loop developing between the art and the observer.

I felt I'd gone far enough when I hit the following quote by Brook Zen: "*Duende*. It dilates the mind's eye, so that the intensity becomes almost unendurable."

On the top of a fresh sheet of paper I wrote:

Duende Checklist

1. Must come from the soul
2. Must embrace both life and death
3. Must be completely original
4. Must be an intense experience that changes both artist and audience

Along with my passport and landing papers, I had my checklist, but I didn't like it. It made *duende* sound boring instead of transcendent. I closed my eyes and tried to find my own personal definition.

I imagined a kind of corkscrew into the head that allowed an experience to enter a person's being and ricochet around her soul, bouncing against the good, the bad, the bright, the dark, in context of with her own life until a new truth is illuminated. She could understand the very pith and core of an emotion as never before. I reread the definition. I liked it. Liked the danger of it.

I also figured that age had to be on my side. *Duende* was not for the young or faint of heart. Surely, only an older person understands seriously that death is part of even the brightest day.

Three days later, I sat in the sun at a small metal table in Seville's

Plaza de la Alfalfa, feeling pleasantly a part of the place. I liked the plaza's unassuming workman-like vibe. Families were packed tight around me, enjoying their Saturday. Lively chatter flowed. Kids of all ages filled the plaza, running in and out of the trees, lazing on mother's or father's laps. Others huddled in groups, heads touching, sharing secrets. It was a bright scene. A happy scene. No skulking *duende* that I could see. Just well-cared-for kids, animated adults enjoying a meal in an impeccably clean square.

Still, the question continued to haunt me. Why do the Spanish have *duende*? Why have they've created a new word and a whole cult around this force?

I remembered a passage in James Michener's book *Iberia* where he said that to tell a Spanish person that she has *duende* was the highest compliment possible. I struggled to imagine any other culture where this would be so. What would be the supreme compliment you could give an American? You're going places? You've lost weight?

A night later I was sure I'd encountered *duende* at last, when during dinner, a mournful dirge of horns and drums filled the night. I ran to the street, thinking I'd find a funeral procession, but there, swaying on a giant float, stood an enormous Jesus dressed in a long black robe, a noose around his neck, a crown of thorns on his head, blood on his face. This was surely the ultimate embrace of death. Death in spades. I followed the procession as it snaked through the narrow streets, my heart lurching to the beat of the bass drum. This parade, dark and deeply Catholic, had everything to do with *duende* and the Spanish soul, but although I found a kind of beauty in the lugubrious march, my mind was not corkscrewed open. Instead, I felt a welling terror at the force of religion.

My week in Seville sped by. I enjoyed the Parque de Maria Luisa, wandered the gardens of the Réal Alcázar, climbed the Giralda, visited Triana, soaked in a *hammam*, ate too many tapas, drank a lot of Rioja, but I was no closer to *duende* than when I'd started. I had not even found it in flamenco music and dance where it reportedly loves to lurk.

By my last full day in Seville, I'd officially given up my search for *duende*. The night before, at a tapas bar, I'd found *Duende* fish on the menu. *That's it*, I thought. *Close enough*. I could joke that I'd found *duende* and had consumed it—leave it at that.

Back at the hotel I searched for *Duende* fish on the Internet. A very ugly creature, it's a type of shark, so named because the fish has a pointed snout that looks like a goblin's hat. I'd come full circle, back to the imp-elf magical creature definition.

The next day, in the fresh morning chill, I felt almost giddy with freedom. The day was mine. I decided to walk the exterior walls of the Réal Alcázar at a fast pace. The notched walls topped with their pointed hats looked like something a young girl dressed in full fairy princess regalia would invent—beautiful, fanciful, but were in fact twelfth-century state of the art defensive walls built by the Moors. I crossed Plaza del Triunfo, faced the Puerto del León, touched the wall and turned left.

Marching a fast pace, I came to the lovely sunny Calle Agua, so named because it was once a Roman aqueduct. Passing Calle Vida, I stopped for a moment to enjoy the intersection of water and life. The ancient Moors would approve. In their world water was sacred, life giving, the very center of existence. After a time the wall veered sharp right onto a small park framed by giant wrought-iron doors. On the left, an enormous ficus tree shaded a stone patio. Straight ahead, a walkway lined with blossoming orange trees filled the air with their dizzying scent and on the right, a blue and white tile planter ran along the outside of the Alcázar's wall. Not a single soul to be seen. I walked through the open gates and down the steps to the patio. Wait, the park was not empty after all.

A girl wearing a polka dot T-shirt tucked into black jeans sat on the planter's edge in the shade of the wall. It struck me as odd that she was alone. The kids here always seemed to be in groups or with family. She was at that age, that poignant cusp of womanhood age, about eleven or twelve. Softly she hummed a flamenco song, almost dreamily clapping the rhythm. I caught her eye, smiled and pantomimed clapping along with her.

Her face darkened. She did not return my smile. I felt I'd intruded. Her body shifted forward on the planter. She sat up straight and placed both sneaker-clad feet firmly on the ground, her gaze focused mid-distance. Her hands, now firm with purpose, clapped a complex rhythm. Her feet pounded the earth at intervals I could not anticipate. Then she sang, her voice a deep clear alto.

Tears sprang to my eyes for this gift. I remembered watching my now grown-up daughter near the same age perform at a dance concert. I'd cried then too. Tears of pride for her accomplishments, for giving it her best. The music shifted. Took on an ominous tone. I looked over to the girl, her face blank, her focus somewhere deep inside and I remembered the dread, the fear that my daughter would not be well. That a darkness lay in wait for her. That her teen years would be like mine. That she would struggle with the despair that had almost drowned me. That she'd slip away unseen from this world. My sorry genetic gift to her.

I looked up at the polka-dot-clad girl, the child-like softness now gone from her face. I know she felt my tears. They became part of the song. How could one so young sing like this? Are some souls born to these dark emotions? Was that a blessing or a curse? I felt the dread rise again. Be well, sweet girl. Find a sunny life.

As suddenly as she'd started, she stopped, crossed her legs and leaned back against the wall. I wiped the tears off my cheeks with the back of my hand. We stared at each other.

"*Mucho duende*," I whispered. "*Gracias.*"

This time she smiled. Hair escaping a messy pony, a smudge of dirt on her sneakers, she became a child again. Just a child. And I embraced the shadowy despairing child within me, understanding for the first time that without the dark there is no light.

The Torre del Oro across a Moonlit Guadalquivir

RIVER RAMBLING IN SEVILLE

Lynne Rutan

Quiet water has always been my balm, so when the Andalusian intoxication with life that explodes from the confines of Seville's narrow cobblestone streets and alleys—the speeding cars squealing around tight corners, the honking motor bikes buzzing pedestrians, the crowds bubbling over with conversation and conviviality into light-filled plazas and dark bodegas—became too much for me, it was time to head to the river.

I love the noise and spirit of the people, whose twenty-first century lives play out in that ancient cityscape. At times, however, the ebullient spirit that draws me in exhausts me. After three days as a tourist, I grew impatient at trying to negotiate the tangle of streets designed by the Moors to confound their enemies, my nose pressed in a map at every tiny intersection and my back pressed against whitewashed walls by the traffic.

As a child, I embraced my family and my studies, but sometimes everything and everyone became just too much. When parents, brothers, and school weighed down my small shoulders, I'd sneak off to a creek just far enough from home to feel I had pulled off an escape. Alone, cooling my heels, the water's gentle flow carried away the pressures of being a nice girl, a good daughter, and an A student. In my travels I still seek out water—a river, a stream, an ocean, a lake, even a pond—to slow the frenzy of exploration while I think about where I've been and where I'm going.

On a cool, blue-sky morning in early March I set out on the wide promenade that hugs the banks of the Guadalquivir River for miles from Seville's docks to a park on the other end of town. It offered an escape from the tight crush of traffic and crowds, a safe haven for pedestrians, dog walkers, bikers, for those awkward Segways, even for parents and kids on their old-fashioned scooters. My goal: to walk a couple of miles upstream to the Puente del Alamillo. The landmark bridge was designed by world-famous Spanish architect Santiago Calatrava to connect the city to the grounds of the 1992 Universal Exposition. During the late '90s, when I lived in Dallas, that city was so seduced by the architect's work, it debated and later built, its own, controversial Calatrava Bridge, with another now in the works. I wanted to see the bridge that had inspired my former city's bridge envy.

The Guadalquivir, for good and evil, has always been Seville's lifeblood. The only great navigable river in Spain, it birthed the city, brought it a fortune beyond imagination, and then nearly killed it. First came the Phoenicians, then the Romans in the second century BCE, building a great port and walled city on the banks of the river then called Baetis. From the Arabic the Moors gave it the modern name, Guadalquivir, meaning "the great river." They also built the watchtower, the Torre del Oro, which today has been reduced to guarding a fleet of sightseeing boats.

In 1492, just down the river from where I walked, Christopher Columbus sailed fifty miles to the Atlantic Ocean and on to the New World. Upon his return, Seville became the only port authorized to trade with the Indies. The designation made it the most important city in the world, home to 200,000 people, and the arrival and departure points for every trans-oceanic voyage.

However, what the river gave, it also took away. The Guadalquivir began to silt up, the plague decimated the population, and after a century and a half of glory, Seville lost its monopoly to Cádiz and slipped into obscurity for more than a hundred years. In the twelfth century a Moorish poet described the river's fickle cruelty: "the west wind ripped the river's tunic, the river overflowed its banks to pursue and take revenge."

It took until the eighteenth century for humans to begin reining in the river's power and unpredictability with re-channeling, canals, and finally a world-famous lock system that limits the tidal ebb and flow. Don't tell *Sevillanos* or many tourist mapmakers, but the placid green sheet of water along which I walked is actually the Canal de Alfonso XIII, a stubby spur of the main river. Residents looked at me askance when I asked the name of the waterway that runs through the city—"Guadalquivir, of course." It took me some musing to decide it didn't matter about the technical stuff that differentiates the river and canal to go with the flow and enjoy the view.

If there are still traces of the river's once capricious power, they weren't in evidence during my stroll. An intermittent breeze ruffled the surface, but the deep green waters were so calm I had to ask a boatman the direction of the current. It appears, as one Moorish poet wrote, that the once mighty river has "shame-faced, crawled back into his bed to hide under its veil."

The tamed river suits its present-day boating traffic. Although the port downriver still handles seagoing vessels, here fragile shells and kayaks from boat houses that dot the banks bear their hardworking rowers inches from the water, undisturbed by the minimal wake of the slow-moving tourist boats. A man biked toward me at full speed, screaming something incomprehensible. I ducked for cover, but as he flew by I realized I wasn't the target. He was keeping pace with and shouting instructions to a crew team cutting through the water. The rowers' perfectly-timed, even strokes operated like a well-oiled engine, propelling the long narrow shells forward.

Across the river, my view changed as I headed upstream from the vibrant palette of Triana's old waterfront buildings to a skyline of futuristic structures from Expo '92 and the Isla Magica amusement park. My eyes were drawn upward by a red oval office tower that dwarfs everything in Seville. Officially it's called the Cajasol Tower, Seville's first thirty-seven-story skyscraper, but its derisive nickname "Lipstick" seemed more appropriate.

High walls keep the city from encroaching on the river. It was hard to believe that traffic jammed a multi-lane highway just above the promenade; down here the road noise was muffled. Water stirred the reeds and lapped against the shoreline. Doves cooed and a few small black water birds cackled among themselves. I could hear the fishermen with their long poles plop their bait in the water and pull out small, flapping fish. The men looked at me, uncomprehending, when I asked if they'd be eating their catch of the day for dinner.

In many places the massive stone blocks of the walls look like they have been in place for centuries, perhaps part of the old city fortifications. Now graffiti artists have commandeered them as a colorful, miles-long outdoor gallery, covering the ancient spaces with vibrant twenty-first century cartoons and pop culture illustrations.

This is not your average gang tagging. I swear a giant eye with long black lashes blinked. A realistic Janet Leigh painted stepping from her shower in *Psycho* could be a photo from the movie. Barn-sized graphics and stylized lettering comment on war and politics. In contrast to the quiet river water, the art shouts its messages, heavy or humorous.

The four bridges beneath which I walked became progressively more modern. The elegant cast-iron arches of the nineteenth century Puente Isabel II connect Seville with Triana, once home to seafarers and gypsies. The canvas tenting of the Puente del Cachorro protects pedestrians from Seville's devastating summer sun. The unassuming Cartuja Bridge serves pedestrians. The Barqueta Bridge, with its steel clean modern arches and distinctive red cables helped welcome the world to Expo '92, to celebrate the 500th anniversary of Columbus's voyage to the New World.

From the Barqueta Bridge I could see at least a part of my destination, the white column of the Alamillo Bridge protruding nearly 500 feet into the cloudless sky. As the city prepared to host the Expo '92, officials also commissioned Calatrava—a neo-futuristic architect, structural engineer, sculptor and painter—to create a bridge that would embody the city's soaring aspirations for the future. From my first sighting—and with apologies to Mae West—I couldn't suppress the question, "Is that the Alamillo Bridge or is Seville just happy to see me?"

Standing on the bridge's elevated walkway, I imagined the world-famous architect in his studio, envisaging a brilliant white, cantilevered column braced by a harp-like triangle of guide wires to represent the prow and riggings of a sailing vessel. It would harken back to Seville's past as a maritime power and project the city proudly forward. Perhaps Calatrava also pictured the column's beak-like top as a seabird, a companion to Columbus or Magellan as they sailed from Seville on their voyages of discovery. However, as built, the 440-foot-long steel column, although sleek and graceful, juts at an awkward angle high above the river and the city, looking like a monumental phallic symbol, at least to me.

To be fair, critics say Calatrava's bridges transform engineering into an art form. City fathers in places like Dallas looked at his work and wanted their own. Despite these accolades, the bridge says to me we are all human; even famous architects make mistakes. The creative genius is the one who turns them into assets.

Passers-by must have wondered at the American woman standing at the base of the bridge's column, craning her neck back, staring up and laughing. I had come to the river for quiet, peaceful reflection and a brief escape from the city. I found some of that, as well as vitality, art and humor—and even some unexpected naughtiness in the city's saucy welcome—perhaps not what I expected, but just what this nice girl really needed.

Walking in Andalusia

My Sevilla: The Streets of Sevilla

For My Fellow Travelers
Thanasis Maskaleris

Daedalos, the arch-labyrinth designer-builder,
would feel envious and inferior,
if he had walked the labyrinthine streets of Seville ...

Walking the streets of Seville leads to continuous wonders;
here are the gateways to the Andalusian culture ...
The names of her streets ring with the past:
her kings, conquerors, dictators, reformers, liberators ...
The street signs shine with the many faces of Christ and
    Virgin Mary—
the hope-givers to humankind ...
Everywhere the present-eternal palpitations of the heart:
musica, amor, alegría, dolor, sueños, flamenco, duende ...
Calle Amador de los Rios—Lover of Rivers Street
Calle de la Salude—Health Street
Calle Andalucia Amarga—Street of Bitter Andalusia
Calle de la Paz—Street of Peace
Calle Hihas de Caridad—Daughters of Charity Street
Calle Sueños—Street of Dreams
Calle Alegría—Street of Joyfulness

Calle Amor—Street of Love
Calle de los Gitanos Sagrados—Street of the Sacred Gypsies

Here the opposite balconies are so close to one another
that Antonio and Lola (all Romeos and Juliets of Seville),
could visit each other with a little jump across the way...

At the Plaza de España

RETRACING SEVILLE

Maryly Snow

He who Seville has not seen
Has not seen a marvel great.
—Popular Spanish Saying

Perhaps it is a thin story, this sliver of my long ago visit to Seville, a tale weighted with a waning romance and an expiring passport, both with just days left in their lives, but when I returned to the Andalusian capital years later, it was these experiences that compelled me to retrace what I remembered of the lovely city.

I can recollect only two places from the Seville I knew forty-two years ago—one darkly, the other with gratitude. I'm not sure which of my two problems was worse: traveling with a passport due to expire ten days before my ticketed return flight home or traveling with an emotionally inaccessible man, however handsome.

I had taken the train to Almería to meet my long-haired hippy travel partner, a man I'd met on the Mikhail Lermontov, a Russian ocean liner. The year was 1974. We were on our way to Morocco. The only problem was my passport had been stolen in Paris. The U.S.

State Department had issued me a temporary passport good for three months, ten days shy of my planned return. I had begged for an extension on repeated visits to the American Embassies in Paris and London where waits in long, impersonal lines yielded only clerks who said, "wait" and "there is nothing we can do."

My partner and I left Almería for Seville to visit its American consulate, hoping against hope that with personal contact someone might extend my passport. Once in that gorgeous, walkable, and friendly city, I realized how inaccessible my travel companion—I'll call him Javier—truly was. I remember brooding in a vast plaza replete with welcoming nooks and crannies adorned with colorful hand-painted tiles while I basked in the December sun and pondered my mistake. Years later I wondered—what was that place?

I also remember standing outside the American consulate, calmed by its well-maintained and handsome Spanish Revival architecture, reminding me a bit of home, of California, while I hoped for a better outcome than from the impersonal American embassies. Inside, I was greeted warmly and ushered into the consul general's office. There I sipped tea from a fine china cup while sitting in an upholstered chair, feeling every inch the lady, feeling, finally, respected by my government. Two days later my passport was extended.

As I prepared for my much-delayed return to Seville, I wondered, what it would be like to visit those places again. Would I recognize them? What would I feel after the interceding passage of four decades?

Before leaving home, Internet searches revealed that I had brooded in the Plaza de España, Spain's primary contribution to the 1929 Ibero-American Exposition in Seville. Seville spent more than a decade readying itself for that expo, widening streets and building hotels. Evidence of that preparation is still extant, but of all of these expo-induced developments, the Plaza de España is perhaps Seville's most popular. It is the second most visited site, the first being the city's other, older heart: the Cathedral and La Giralda, its climbable bell tower, one of only three Almohad minarets in the world.

I had much more trouble locating the American consulate in Seville online. Eventually I contacted the U.S. State Department because the address on the Internet did not jibe with my memory. The consulate where I had sipped tea and received my renewed passport was a grand building near the Plaza de España. It was only after many sends and replies that my emails were forwarded to "consular agent" Alan Campbell in Seville. He knew the history of the consulate. From him I learned that the original building had also been built for the 1929 Ibero-American Exposition, that its architect was William Templeton Johnson, a San Diego architect known for his Spanish Revival buildings. The United States built three exposition buildings, the largest of which, the Pabellon de Estados Unidos, remains standing, as it had been planned all along to become the American Consulate once the expo was over, a function it served until 2006. But in 2006, the consulate was downgraded to a "consular agency," and a staff of thirty shrank to a mere two. It was moved to a second floor office on the Plaza Nueva. That sounded neither familiar nor promising.

When I arrived in Seville that second time, I found it still gorgeous, walkable and friendly. The first place I revisited is Seville's most well known, a stop on every tourist's itinerary, the stunningly grand Plaza de España. What did I feel now, forty-two years later, upon seeing the plaza? Awe. Just plain unadorned awe. I gazed across the half-a-million square feet of plaza with its three entrance towers, the center one a tall, ornate portal and its wide green moat surrounding the serpentine-paved island at its center. The hand-painted tiles (*azulejos*) of my memory were everywhere: inside the long shaded semi-circle, covering every inch of the forty-nine benches and shelves of the Alcoves of the Provinces; shining on the blue and white ceramic balusters supporting the balustrades of the moat's four bridges. I sat again, this time soaking up the March sun, in an alcove named Almería, the province and city where I should have heeded the cooling embers of my old romance. Curiously, the tiles of the forty-nine provinces depict mostly rural scenes—ox-pulled carts or peasants dancing in local dress. Early twentieth-century city life and architecture are strangely absent from these tiles. The location of each province within Spain is shown on a large ceramic map embedded in the floors of all the provincial alcoves, like living room rugs. Cubbyholes on the sides of each alcove originally held local newspapers to make Spain known to itself. I'm pretty sure I didn't know anything about the 1929 Exposition when I first lounged there, probably never noticed the large glazed historical medallion set in the pavement. Today the place is thronged with visitors armed with selfie-sticks, the cubbyholes empty.

The old American Consulate once stood a few blocks away. This place had especially symbolized for me the graciousness of Spain. I knew now that it had become the Fundación Valetín de Madaraiga y Oya, with some relationship to modern art. It would be my next stop in retracing my first visit to Seville.

I crossed over from the wide river-fronting Paseo de Cristóbal Colón to where it changed its name to the Paseo de las Delicias and continued almost to the Puente de los Remedios. There it was, the handsome Spanish Revival building of my memory. The two-story red banner proclaimed "Centro de Arte Contemporáneo." I stood stupidly at its entrance gate. Locked! Litter underfoot, as if no one cared, no one visited. Next door stood a Sevillian tourist office, housed in the tiny striped Costurero de la Reina (aka the Queen's Sewing Box, built in 1893). I asked about the Fundación.

"Oh, they open and close whenever they want," came the offhand response. "They don't seem to have a regular schedule."

Stammering, I replied, "But ... I saw open windows on the second

112

floor, even though the entrance seems unused," as I pointed back toward the Paseo.

"Ah, the entrance is over there, on Avenida de Maria Luisa."

"Oh." I walked to the Avenida. This façade there exactly duplicated the other one, but here the lock on the gate looked newer, the walkway unlittered. This side also sported a two-story banner, a blue one proclaiming "Centro de Arte Contemporáneo." Gate locked, no sign of posted hours, I stood there dumbfounded. A locked center of contemporary art with no hours?

That's when a young woman appeared. She looked at me with gentle curiosity, then opened the gate.

"Oh, it's open," I sputtered.

"Of course." She smiled. "Would you like to go in?"

I said I did, explaining that I had been here many years ago and wanted to see the place again. She had to go inside to ask permission, returning with a *yes*.

Inside, a guard seemed to have nothing to do as there was no one else around. The young woman showed me where the exhibition was, and what was off-limits. She, an intern with an undergraduate degree in art history, had started work there only a week before. After we parted I wandered, alone, through the MP Collection of Contemporary Art, a sequence of near empty rooms with blackout shades over the windows, dim lighting, an absence of color, the only visitor myself. How strange, I thought again as I viewed pieces by many of the 20th century's contemporary art stars: Carl Andre, Josef Beuys, Bernd & Hilla Becher, Christo, Olafur Eliasson, Vik Muniz, Robert Smithson, James Turrell and Andy Warhol, and five unfamiliar Spanish names: Ibon Aranberri, Federico Guzmán, Cristina Iglesias, Gonzalo Puch, and MP & MP Rosado. The fountain in the central patio was shrouded in thick plastic, wrapped with rope and surrounded by broken unglazed ceramic vessels. It is not a temporary installation piece because the Fundación's own brochure shows the fountain unwrapped, running with water. *How strange*, I thought again. My memory of a cup of tea in an upholstered chair remained unsatisfied, replaced by a new, stranger reality.

From there I walked to America's "consular agency" in Plaza Nueva. No American flag flew outside. It was marked by a small plaque among six others and a man on the sidewalk who turned out to be a security guard without a uniform. The entrance seemed as nondescript as possible, the result of a downsizing five years after 9-11, precipitated, perhaps, by the need for a cloak of invisibility combined with cost cutting.

I walked up the narrow stairs to a locked, alarmed, security-camera-ed, peep-hole door. Once buzzed inside the small lobby (all of six chairs) I waited a long while for the clerk to get a receipt for her one customer's passport payment.

"It's taking a long time," I said to the customer.

"It's always that way," she replied.

Finally, my turn. I explained to the female receptionist why I was there, the whole story, and that the consular agent Alan Campbell had invited me to view the plaque listing all the previous consul generals. That's when the clerk, Jackie, introduced herself. She had been employed in Seville's American Consulate since 1963. She must have waited on me! Then Alan Campbell came out, dressed casually in pressed chinos and a polo shirt, carrying a wooden plaque with rows of brass name plates, explaining that the hanging wire had broken several months previously and they hadn't gotten around to re-hanging it yet.

The consul who offered me tea in 1974 was named Curtis Campbell, a man Jackie said knew everyone in Seville. When he held a function at the consulate, she said, "all of Seville turned out." I felt such nostalgia, knowing this tiny office, staff of two, Jackie and Alan, could not hope to match the prestige of the agency's earlier incarnation, a feeling heightened when Alan's golden retriever, Rover, bounded up to join them at the counter. I was glad, on the one hand, that the American government was saving money, but rueful, on the other, at the loss of its grandeur and prestige, its need for security in its semi-secrecy. When I left, I kept turning around, looking back, thinking maybe I hadn't just emerged from a consular hole in the wall.

But things do change. The elusive and ultimately empty romance that brought me to Seville in the first place has long faded; the expiring passport problem, too, reduced to a spec of time. I knew all along that I'd conflated my gratitude toward the consul general in the stately American Consulate to the entire city of Seville. In retracing my steps, my distant memories remained brief events, now unimportant, but the city itself shone brightly: friendly, accessible, graceful, full of warm people generous of spirit and new, far less ghostly, experiences.

Wedding Veil in Shop Window

Sevilla: Our Lady of the Veil

Rita Gardener

Sevilla, you are
a small storefront in a winding alley.
Your roll-up doors open like eyelids
in the mid-morning sun
as nearby church bells ring,
reveal
the bride-to-be in virginal white,
the wedding veil
next to the mannequin
in the transparent camisole
strategically open to reveal
a lacy thong, a bare thigh.

Strappy stilettos, also white,
strike a provocative pose
atop the bridal train.
Shoppers, voyeurs,
pass by,
slip in, buy
or don't.
Some of them stop

at the baby goods shop
displaying an infant
in a white flamenco dress.
Church bells mark the hours as shadows deepen,
the taverns empty
the last patron departs
and the rolling doors pull down,
touch the cheekbone of the street.
Graffiti smudged eyelids
gray and purple with messages—
indiscernible, secret.

Who are you now
behind lids closed until
the dove's soft mourn
pulls the night into dawn
when once again
those lids raise
to the sunshine,
the swelling buds on the orange trees
and the calls to prayer,
ready again
to lift the veil?

Christopher Columbus

REDISCOVERING COLUMBUS

Rita Gardener

It was late morning in Seville when I met up with Christopher Columbus in the majestic Santa Metropolitana Patriarcal Iglesia Catedral de Sevilla. This would not be the first time I'd communed with the noted admiral. As the tour guide pointed to his tomb with reverence, I silently thought, *His supposed tomb.* Columbus and I go way back, you see. Our many encounters took place in what is now the Dominican Republic, on the Caribbean island of Hispaniola. In 1492, after Columbus famously made landfall following his first ocean journey, he christened the land *La Española* (Hispaniola) and built the city of Santo Domingo. And that is where, sixty years ago, I first met Cristóbal Colón, as he's known in the Spanish-speaking world. He was safely ensconced in Santo Domingo's cathedral, on the same island my family had made their own.

While we lived on a rural coconut farm on the country's north shore, our yearly trips to the bright lights of Santo Domingo included trips to the Alcázar, Columbus's ancient Spanish fort constructed to protect the city from marauders. I still remember the hush and faint salty smell of the cathedral, built of coral limestone. I absorbed the coolness of the dusty interior and the echoes of history suspended in the air like dust motes. I breathed in Columbus's presence in that oldness; it became somehow part of me even as we stepped back outside to the hot tropical sun and journeyed across the mountains to our farm.

As I stood in Seville's cathedral in 2016, the waves of history crashed around me in that darkened place of worship, and I felt heavy with the weight. I paused at the high altar, a garish display of gilded woodcarvings, the gold plundered from the New World by Columbus and all the mariners that followed in the ensuing centuries. The altar's ornate carvings depict the life of Christ. There is no depiction here of the price paid for these glittering treasures. All I could think about was the lives and cultures lost by the thirst for gold, for the right to claim a new land for Spain, and the imposition of a new religion. This gold came from the New World: from Hispaniola and its neighbors.

Hispaniola was the land of the Taino people before the Spanish invasion plundered the island and changed the course of its history overnight. I grew up in the Dominican Republic, knowing this dark story, and how Columbus and his followers enslaved the Tainos to work in gold mines. Weakened and felled by foreign diseases, forced labor and killings, few natives were left alive within forty years of Columbus's conquests. While Seville's coffers were being filled with gold, the Tainos were disappearing. But they are not forgotten. In the Dominican village where I grew up, the Tainos are like spirits flickering in and out of stories told by the elders, and by words still used today all over the world: *Hurricane* is derived from a word meaning "god of the storm." *Caribbean* comes from a Taino word for human being. It's impossible to ignore the many other examples derived from the native islanders, such as *tobacco, maize, canoe*, and *hammock*. My friends' forefathers had Taino blood. Objects from the ancient days were passed along to their descendants. One of my childhood friends still used a large earthenware water jug, a Taino artifact handed down through the generations by her great-great-grandmother.

Gold still exists on Hispaniola. A rural hamlet near our coconut farm was called La Mina, a word which means "the mine." As a child, I used to pan the streams that flowed through our property from the hills in La Mina and find flecks of gold. Locals showed us nuggets they'd collected over the years, or gold coins that surfaced from shipwrecks. Columbus's own flagship *Santa Maria* ran aground on Christmas Day in 1492 somewhere off the coast of Hispaniola. It has yet to be located. Just a few years ago an explorer found a wreck that archeologists thought might be that vessel, but in 2015 it was found to be a different one. Even so, the island's waters are full of the bones of ships lost to storms as they headed back to Spain with their plunder. Modern-day bounty hunters still search Dominican bays for shipwrecks and treasure. And so the connections to the Old and New Worlds continue, interpreted variously. A thin thread of history separates viewpoints between Seville and the New World, including the truth about Columbus's final resting place.

So you might understand my skepticism as I stood in in Seville's cathedral in 2016, as a tide of people surged and ebbed around me. This sea lapped up against the velvet ropes, anxious to view the large tomb held aloft by life-sized bearers representing Spain's four kingdoms during the navigator's life. I strained to hear our guide in the din. The gist of her narration asserted that this, indeed, is the noted navigator's final resting place. She cited tests in the early 2000s performed by a team of Spanish geneticists on slivers of bones inside the tomb. These results were compared with DNA from Columbus's brother Diego, also buried in Seville. They were declared a match and proof that the contents of the mausoleum are indeed his.

The team of geneticists did concede that even though they are convinced the bones in Seville are Columbus's, it doesn't rule out the possibility that the bones in Santo Domingo also belong to the discoverer of the New World. Since our man Columbus continued to travel extensively for centuries after his death, parts and pieces of his bones could, conceivably, also be elsewhere. Spain has long desired that the Dominican government conduct tests of the tomb contents in Santo Domingo to settle the battle of the bones once and for all. The Dominicans have refused, saying it is un-Christian to bother the dead. Not that they didn't disturb Columbus at all. His tomb was moved in 1992 a few miles away to a new mausoleum built for the 500th anniversary of Columbus's first voyage. In any case, the Dominican government continues to insist the mariner's bones have never left the island.

So where *is* Columbus today? That may never be known. A summary of his post-death journeys is both enlightening and confusing. Some facts are undisputed. He died in 1506 in Valladolid in Spain. A few years later, his remains traveled to a monastery across the river from Seville. About thirty years later, a daughter-in-law sent his bones to Santo Domingo along with her husband's. Apparently Columbus had wanted to be buried in the Americas but no church of sufficient stature there had existed before the 1530s; thus the long wait for his return voyage. In 1795 Spain was forced to give up Hispaniola to France. So that Columbus wouldn't fall into the victor's hands, the Spaniards shipped his remains from Santo Domingo to Havana, Cuba. A hundred years later, when the Spanish-American War broke out, those remains were transported back to Seville to be entombed in its grand cathedral.

But the story doesn't necessarily end there. Back in Santo Domingo, the government insisted they still had Columbus. They cited a discovery in the late 1800s by workers toiling in the cathedral who unearthed a chest of bones and some writings proclaiming them to be those of none other than the illustrious Cristóbal Colón. Their conclusion: Some other poor soul's bones had been carted off to Cuba and eventually shipped to Seville. Numerous historians and researchers continue the debate about the final, final, resting place. Spain continues to press for DNA testing of the bones in the Dominican Republic, and tourists continue to flock to both countries to be led by guides through the respective mausoleums and told each nation's version of the story.

At least my own Spanish adventure had brought me once again closer to the man. While in Andalusia, he was impossible to escape. I was bombarded with images and stories about him. In a Moorish-tiled great room at the Alhambra ruins in Granada, I walked in his footsteps. It was there that Queen Isabella and King Ferdinand met with the explorer in January 1492. Spain had just defeated the Moors in Granada, and so the monarchs were now able to sponsor Columbus's trip to discover a sea route to Asia. His first ships were built in Andalusia, and sailed away from Spain that same year on their misguided search.

At Seville's Indian Archives, I beheld portraits of Columbus and copies of his signature on documents from Santo Domingo. By the time I left Seville, I had to confess maybe, just maybe, I'd once again gotten close to his remains. Or not. Bones continue to hold secrets and DNA and mysteries. Columbus wanted to be buried, not in Spain, but on the island he conquered. He seemed to want to belong there, much as my family wanted to belong to the island they had adopted as home. But history doesn't grant us all our wishes; as humans we scatter or are scattered, conquer or are conquered. While alive, we are the containers of our bones, but I suspect that our spirits don't care where our corporeal bodies end up, and I like to think that Cristóbal Colón, the Admiral of the Seas, is at peace no matter how the matter of his bones is—or isn't—settled.

The Alhambra

Visions of the Red Castle

Unity Barry

Ancient Arabic poets called the cluster of red palaces and fortresses in Granada, "a pearl set in the middle of emeralds." Now a World Heritage Site, it once glowed as the last outpost of the Arabic empire, then abandoned for hundreds of years, fell into ruins housing outlaws. Its walls witnessed the defeat of the Moors in Spain by Spanish Monarchs Ferdinand and Isabella. Washington Irving wrote the first international bestseller, *Tales of the Alhambra* after living there. The Alhambra blends everything into a dream. I went there to capture some of its magic.

Disgorged from our bus in the parking lot, I became part of the 2.4 million tourists a year who swarm over the hill named al-Sabika, or "crown" in Arabic. My group of writers met our guide who led us up a cypress-bordered lane in our stroll to the Generalife, the Alhambra's gardens set amid tranquil courtyards. Inside each plaza, rugged stone exteriors give way to plants, architecture and decoration calculated to bring spiritual calm to sultans ruling during treacherous times—or perhaps to help treacherous sultans rule with calm calculation.

As we listened to our guide recount the history and tales of the Alhambra, it became clear that fact and fiction have merged into a colorful blur. Upon hearing such tales, my historical fiction writer's imagination frequently turns into a virtual time machine, and I suddenly found myself witnessing the scene.

One sultan—no one agrees which one—discovered his favorite wife was having an affair with a knight from the large and noble Abencerrajes family, but he could not find out which one had turned him into a cuckold. Some say the illicit romance was a fiction, whispered in the ear of the sultan by a rival noble family. As I closed my eyes, I imagined the unknown Muslim monarch from a distant century walking where we stood …

The sultan paces the paths bordering lazy streams that burble along narrow channels. The music of the fountains helps push the pain of fierce emotion behind a curtain in his mind, leaving him as sharp as a scimitar to plan. He summons his most trusted lieutenant and tells him to invite all thirty-seven knights of the Abencerrajes family to a banquet.

On the evening of the celebration, the men arrive at the palace gates in the glow of a setting sun that turns the castle's reddish walls to a brilliant orange. The gold and silver embroidery on the men's robes gleams in the firelight coming from braziers placed as if meant to dazzle the eyes. Their horses are arch-necked Arabians that stamp their hooves from pride in serving such prestigious aristocrats.

After grooms lead away the valuable steeds, the boisterous men are ushered into the palace, but they fail to notice the door locking behind them or the men hiding in the shadows.

A shriek like no other rises from the Courtyard of the Lions and echoes off the floors and walls. The screams of soldiers advancing on their prey joins with the screams of victims. In an instant the sumptuous evening pivots, turning the moment of prestige into a black hell. All the Abencerrajes family cavaliers lie in crumpled heaps, their black-red blood covering the floor and seeping into the marble.

Someone called my name and I returned to the twenty-first century with a jolt to follow our group as we craned our necks to see vast overhead ceilings covered in carvings, some painted in repetitive designs of brilliant colors, and some gilded, in the Throne Room of the Comares Palace. Ceramic tiles cover walls and floors—all in abstract patterns that appear everywhere and seem to dance. All around us, arabesques twirl on walls in yellowing white bas-relief. Some tile patterns have Stars of David laced amid the intricacies. Some are placed adjacent to quotes from the Koran.

Before the *Reconquista* in the fifteenth century, though, the guide told us, for hundreds of years Muslims, Jews and Christians lived and worked side by side on the Iberian Peninsula. Each contributed their unique art to the miraculous Red Castle and other Moorish cities, until King Ferdinand and Queen Isabella issued decrees that all Muslims and Jews must either convert to Christianity or leave Spain.

We arrive in another courtyard where there is more trickling water. The aquatic music transports me, once again, to the past, to the Moors with their desert roots, for whom water attained a mystical beauty that became part of their esthetics.

As I lapse into the theater of my mind, a scene appears filled with harsh soldiers' cries, the rattle and creaking of overloaded carts, and the chaos of a victorious army entrenching itself. Cross-adorned banners snap in the stiff winter wind blowing off the snowy Sierra Nevada. A lone man with arms crossed against the cold, walks up the rocky path to the castle and fortress on top of the hill. Red dust from his journey coats his black breaches and leggings. Under his arm he carries a leather map case. As he nears the stone walls and towers at the hilltop, he stops to catch his breath and brush off his clothes, gazing at the valley and town below. The roads and lanes seem to writhe in the pandemonium of refugees, advancing horses, supply

129

carts and soldiers accosting screaming women.

A guard emerges from the Moorish arch of the fortress gate, his hand on his sword hilt, challenging the man.

"I am Captain Cristóbal Colón. The Christian Monarchs expect me."

Captain Colón thinks of the many long months he had waited while Ferdinand and Isabella defeated the Moors, pushing them out of Europe. The king and queen had assured him that they would give him their answer as soon as peace returned. Cristóbal thinks of how difficult it had been when the monarchs of Portugal, Genoa, England and Venice all had refused his appeal. He takes a deep breath, straightens his coat and tells himself that this time it will be different.

The sea captain follows a soldier through rooms of unparalleled ornamentation. His eyes scan the walls, ceilings and floors, all adorned with richly elaborate designs. Flaming brass braziers provide islands of warmth in the icy rooms. In the Hall of the Ambassadors he sweeps his hat from his head and bows deeply toward Queen Isabella sitting on her throne. The queen is visibly tired. The lines on her face attest to her active leadership battling the heathen Moors. When she speaks, her voice echoes off the tile walls as she tells Captain Colón that, after considerable study, the king and she have decided not to finance his westward voyage. Cristóbal seems to shrink in profound disappointment.

The captain hides his shaking hands. Taking a chance that he will anger the queen, he tells her that he understands how empty their Christian Majesties' treasury must be and points to the vast fortune just waiting for them in the Orient—a fortune large enough to fill the royal coffers. If Ferdinand and Isabella don't take the risk of sailing around the globe to reach the riches of Asia, someone else will, probably King Henry of England or King Charles of France.

Isabella retorts in a sharp voice that the academic men who studied his proposal reviewed the ancient Greek calculations carefully. With a dismissive gesture, she concludes the interview with the pronouncement that Captain Colón has greatly underestimated the globe's circumference. Ships cannot begin to hold the amount of food and water needed for such a long journey.

When Cristóbal opens his mouth to counter with another point, Isabella summons her guards. King Ferdinand and some of his military advisors pass Colón as the queen's soldiers escort the captain toward the palace gate. With a probing look, the king enters the throne room to take his place next to his wife.

Once pushed out of the fortress onto the steep lane down the hill, Cristóbal straightens his hat, squares his shoulders and begins the descent. The view of the craggy mountains, verdant plains and town below elude his notice. Which royal court should he approach now? His mind is such a tumult of problems that he doesn't notice the hoof beats of a horse galloping from behind.

"Captain Colón!" Cristóbal turns to see Ferdinand pulling hard on the reins of his huge warhorse. The captain sinks on one knee in front of the impatiently stomping animal.

The king dismounts easily, then while leading his horse, he and the captain walk side by side away from the astonished crowd. The king confesses that he fears their new realm may soon falter without gold to run the country. He can't offer much money but thinks the risk of this wild scheme is worth the reward. The king promises to pressure wealthy merchants and nobility who are beholden to the Monarchy—so Captain Colón will get his ships. Cristóbal crosses himself then thanks God and his Christian Majesty. He raises his eyes to the Alhambra. It's January 1492—a pivotal year to change the world and his fortune.

A fellow writer gave me a nudge, bringing me back to the present. I needed to keep up with the group; otherwise I'd miss seeing the Alcazaba, the fortified portion of the Alhambra. As I negotiated the treacherously rocky steps and paths through and around the many fortified buildings, I thought about Christopher Columbus and the falsehoods promulgated about him by the American writer and first American Ambassador to Spain, Washington Irving.

In his book, *The Life and Voyages of Christopher Columbus*, Irving spread the myth that Europeans believed the world was flat and that Columbus mainly wanted to prove his theory that the world is an orb. I suspect the fiction writer side of Irving wanted to amp up the excitement in a dull read. A novelist's proclivity I could understand.

In fact, in Columbus's time, all the monarchs of Europe employed well-educated men schooled in mathematics and ancient Greek knowledge. The monarchs themselves were also educated to the highest standards of the day. Many knew the world is round—the only point in dispute was exactly how far around it is.

I wondered about Irving and his inclination to play with fact. But, standing where he stood and seeing through his eyes when he first beheld the Alhambra in 1829, I could suddenly see him too…

Irving sits astride his horse and strokes the ancient stones and flaking mortar with his fingertips. Buildings across from him shimmy in the Andalusian heat. His horse, his Rocinante, leans into the crumbling building seeking shade, while the American stares at a pile of ochre-colored rocks heaped in a corner, as if buttressing the building. A partially collapsed roof attests to earthquakes that forced its abandonment as a palace and fortress. Black fire-stained walls prove the stories of past gypsy and "contrabandista" encampments.

Waving his arm in a wide arc over the clustered stone towers and walls that bristle atop al-Shabika hill, he asks his guide Mateo, "Are you certain this is Doña Antonia-Molina's home? This seems too decrepit for such a duenna with such a dominion. I'd expect more palatial apartments for the governor."

Mateo's smiling face glows in the late spring sun, which also highlights the grime and wear on his rust-colored cloak. The writer dismounts and nods to his guide, who calls himself "The Son of the Alhambra." The man, wearing pauper's rags, had gained Irving's employment by boasting of the many histories he learned as a small child from his hundred-year-old grandfather.

"Señor Irving, do not be fooled by outside appearances. Tia Antonia lives in a beautiful part of the palace. She'll love showing you around."

"Well then, let's meet the esteemed lady."

Mateo raps a massive iron doorknocker on iron-studded ancient wood, the pounding blows echoing off nearby walls. Free roaming chickens squawk in feather-flying alarm. Goats scramble away, hooves clattering on marble-paved pathways. A girl with the olive skin, raven hair and sparkling brown eyes of her long-ago Arabic ancestors opens the door.

Mateo doffs his cap. "*Buenos dias, señorita.* This gentlemen wishes to speak with your aunt."

Irving gazes with delight at the comely girl. She somehow manages to be both demure and saucy at the same time. The aunt appears, wearing a black lace mantilla draped over a gigantic tortoiseshell comb.

"Señorita Molina, I'm an American writer gathering stories for my next book. The governor graciously offered me the use of his apartment in the palace and assured me that you could help. I need a quiet place to live and work."

Tia Antonia smiles, causing her face to crinkle into a web of fine lines. "Welcome Señor, please come in out of the heat. After you've rested, I'll show you everything!"

The writer passes into the splendor of a Moorish courtyard appearing as if the resident sultan has just left. Cooling water splashes in a tiled fountain centered in the square space. Potted plants fill the open air with floral scents.

The niece smiles and flutters her black lace fan while Irving quenches his thirst. He has found a rich source of history, full of romance and oriental exoticism. He has found the place to let his imagination revive many ghosts of ages past. He has found paradise.

That evening, on our bus back to Seville, the sights and sounds of the day played in my mind. I considered Irving, who, like me, told stories that merge truth with folklore and fantasy. I thought about how his many stories turned dusty history into magical visions of the past. As the sun set, I drifted off to sleep, like a modern Scheherazade tired after a long day of weaving my own tales of the Alhambra.

The Alhambra with Sierra Nevadas

THE ALHAMBRA
IN FOUR PLUS MOVEMENTS

Gayle McGill

Prelude—Largo

Long before I'd seen Andalusia I'd heard it. Heard it for years, decades even, coming from the left corner of my living room in the Oakland Hills as my husband attempted to master the classical guitar.

There were days when I had to shout, "Please, I beg of you. Stop that infernal plucking." But over time, flashes of melody took shape. Musical phrases of intense beauty emerged. Two pieces in particular captured my imagination, "Granada," the tone poem by Isaac Albéniz, suffused with a sense of passionate yearning, and "Recuerdos de la Alhambra" (Memories of the Alhambra) by Francisco Tárrega with its shimmering tremolo. I set my sights on visiting Andalusia. I wanted to see the place that had inspired such magical music. In the spring of 2016, I got my chance.

On a gentle March day, I stood in the shadow of the Giralda, once a minaret, now the bell tower for Seville's enormous cathedral. This place was especially meaningful to me. Here, in 1546, Alonso Mudarra, the appointed canon, collected and published the earliest surviving music for the instrument that would become the classical guitar or Spanish guitar.

It is fitting that the guitar got its start in Andalusia, for the instrument seems best able to capture the soul of Spain, and although composers of many nationalities have written for the classical guitar, the Spanish and their diaspora have a love and feel for the instrument that is acknowledged worldwide.

As I wandered around the perimeter of the cathedral and near the Réal Alcázar, a guitarist sat on a raised stone ledge skillfully making his way through another Albéniz tone poem: "Sevilla." Albéniz, born in the late nineteenth century, was a child prodigy who studied and toured with Franz Liszt. On breaks from his European tours he took trains to the various cities in Andalusia and in each place wrote an evocative piano piece infused with local folk melodies and color. There was a connection between Albéniz and his contemporary, the guitarist Tárrega. Tárrega, after running away from home in his early teens to join a gypsy band in Valencia, became a world renowned solo guitarist and was, in fact, the first to transcribe Albéniz's pieces for the guitar.

On that peaceful morning I stood off to the side and listened. The tune "Sevilla" always made me think of a matron, richly dressed, dancing a refined, almost regal dance. I stooped and placed a two-Euro coin in the open guitar case. Yes, Albéniz's "Sevilla" was lovely just like the city it's named for, but I longed to get to Granada and its Alhambra. All that stood between me and this goal was a three-hour bus ride.

The wake-up call came at brutally dark 5:30 a.m. The night before, I'd pulled the Granada and Alhambra pages out of two guidebooks. I looked them over on the bus and knew the day would be fine when I read, "The guitarist Andrés Segovia described Grenada as a 'place of dreams, where the Lord put the seed of music in my soul.'" What an excellent musical start for the day.

I had studied Granada and its fort, the Alhambra, done my homework like a good musician who practices long hours so that the music soars unimpeded. I expected a complex interplay of setting, architecture, gardens and water. I knew, for example, that Granada

138

was the last Moorish state in Spain, and in 1492, when King Boabdil lost it to the Catholic Monarchs, Isabella and Ferdinand, more than six hundred years of continuous Moorish rule came to an end. I knew that the Alhambra contained the best of Moorish architecture and that the Nasrid dynasty had created the exquisite palaces. That the Patio de los Leones courtyard was designed using the golden mean. That its plaza was dissected by four rills in the classic Persian *chahar bagh* design. That the stalactite ceiling of the Sala de los Abencerrajes is said be in inspired by the Pythagorean Theorem. That impressive engineering brought water from the Sierra Nevada to hundreds of cisterns, pools and fountains found in every corner of the fort. I knew these things, and now I needed to let them go. For I had not come for these facts and figures, I had come for the music.

First Movement—Andante
The chilly morning was overcast, misty. I entered the Alhambra, meandered up a wide path lined with cypresses and immediately heard the fall of water. A large feeder stream flowed down through a forest in a stone-lined channel then disappeared under the path— Sierra melt water topped up by recent rains. Slowly, savoring each step, I wandered the Jardines del Portal with its tidy parterres filled with tulips, snapdragons, lilies and iris. Small rills brimming with water bordered the path. I stopped in a horseshoe-shaped stand of mature cypresses, their tops grown together forming a solid mass. A secret place. A not-on-the-tour place. On the ground a small lotus-shaped fountain softly burbled a counterpoint to the song of birds. I lifted my face to the mist and shut my eyes. A breeze hummed through the cypress and there, far off, more water, echoes of water in all directions. Moving water sounded the beat that held this beautiful place together.

From my spot, I had a view of most of the Alhambra and its surrounding walls. The mist obscured the city of Granada below and the Sierra Nevada above. The fort seemed to float untethered on the clouds. Huddled tour groups dotted the scene. How lucky was I to be alone in this secret place with the achingly beautiful music of "Granada" running through my head?

Second Movement—Allegro
High noon. I waited in line to enter the Nasrid Palacio complex. The morning had cleared revealing the snow-laden Sierra. I couldn't help but look over at the Palacio de Carlos built by Ferdinand and Isabella. If that building were music it would be the dissonant blat of a hundred tubas gone out of tune. On the other hand, the Nasrid Palacios are said to be seductively beautiful. I smiled remembering a scene from Woody Allen's *Vicki Cristina Barcelona*. Spanish guitar can be seductive too. In the scene, Vicky (Rebecca Hall), a very sensible and about-to-be-married woman, upon hearing a guitar version of "Granada" in the warm Spanish night decides that it is a fine idea to lie down in the bushes and make love with an almost stranger, Juan Antonia (Javier Bardem). Of course, given it was Javier Bardem, "Mary Had a Little Lamb" might have done the trick.

The line moved. I loved the way I was led through a dark hall, then a sharp right down a ramp to a small door—the sense of anticipation building. The Moors understood that delayed pleasure is the keenest, like that slight hesitation in music, that silence between the notes that leaves you begging for the coming dazzle of melody. And suddenly, I entered the blazing light of the first patio.

Dizzy with beauty, I whirled from patio, to palace, to garden, to courtyard, to portico almost undone by the scale of the tile work, delicacy of latticed arches, the trill of water and the almost unbearable lightness of the marble in the sun.

I rested in the shaded end of the Patio de los Leones to collect myself. I imagined Tárrega in this most beautiful of courtyards

composing the first A minor portion of "Recuerdos de la Alhambra."
He would have started with the tremolo.

A tremolo is a single note played by the ring, middle and index
finger in rapid succession with the melody played by the thumb. It
gives the music a shimmering quality that is sustained throughout the entire piece just like water flowing through the Alhambra.
Some hearing the composition for the first time think that there
must be two guitars playing—that there is more gorgeous music
wedged into the composition than a single guitarist could possibly
produce. The patio felt the same way to me. The solo guitar captured
the complexity of the square perfectly. A full symphony would
overwhelm.

Slowly, with great pleasure, I let the space seep through me. The
ambiance was one of exquisite grace. I lingered on the gentle sound
of the lion fountain, the slight rush of the rills that dissected the
courtyard into quadrants. Like chords moving toward resolution, the
delicate patio carried a strong architectural punch that reflected the
Islamic ideals of harmony, symmetry, pattern and order—the same
principles that could be used to describe a perfect musical
composition like "Recuerdos de la Alhambra."

Third Movement—Grave
Completely dazzled, I headed to the Alcazaba, the military area and
the oldest part of the Alhambra. Time to climb the massive Torre de
la Vela. The views of Granada, the mountains and back across the
Alhambra from the top were stunning. This must be the true setting
for Albéniz's "Granada." I thought of Boabdil, the last Moorish King
of Granada, surrendering the keys to the kingdom to Ferdinand and
Isabella and turned to look back at the palaces lost to him. This was
the end of the Moors in Spain. The aching beauty of the Albéniz's
music made absolute sense to me.

Albéniz who had a nostalgic fascination with ancient Spain and fancied himself of Moorish descent, called the piece a heartbreaking lament. I knew that Puerto del Suspiro del Moro (Pass of the Moor's Sigh) could be seen from this spot. Legend has it that Boabdil looking back on Granada and the Alhambra wept and let out a sigh heard far across the Mediterranean to North Africa. I hummed the three-note-descending phrase that is repeated again and again at the end of Albéniz's composition. Surely, this is the last sigh of the Moor.

Fourth Movement—Allegro

I turned away from the view and music in a minor key and moved toward the hopeful sounds of the second portion of "Recuerdos de la Alhambra" in C major. I had saved what I hoped was the best for last—the Generalife (Architect's Garden). I now thought of the water as tremolo. Always present. Always leading. I followed the water—sought out its music.

The elevation increased and from the rose-filled lower garden I got the first views looking back at the Alhambra. The light had started to bend, giving the walls a pinkish tinge. Glorious. Was it this view that inspired Tárrega to move the music to a major key?

Steps and more steps like an ascending chromatic scale. I imagined the music with its shining tremolo pushing me forward. I heard the splash and babble of water as I entered the Patio de la Acequia. I took in the beauty of the fountains shooting their arched streams into a long narrow channel lined by bedding plants. I walked the length of the pool, feeling the sparkle of water on my face. Mountain breezes sang through the shinning white portico at the end. I found a small staircase to the left and climbed yet higher toward the aggressive reverberation of water flowing in the Patio de la Sultana. This was surely the climax of the music, of the place. I reveled in the pattern, the repetition, and yet the originality of each pool and fountain.

But no, not done. A steep stairway lined the very edge of the garden—the Escalera de Agua. At its base a huge lotus-shaped fountain set into an intricately tiled floor exuberantly beckoned, but it was the staircase itself that amazed. The balustrades were not railings but rills filled to the brim with water barely under control, crashing down the steep staircase. I climbed, buoyed by the whoosh of water: every ten steps or so another landing, another gushing fountain. Splendid. My heart pounded to the water's beat. My feet moved at a presto pace. I defied the gravity thrusting the water down and continued to rise.

Finale—Vivace

My boots soaked through. My sweater dampened. My hair went to frizz. Years ago, I'd asked an Indian friend why the women in Bollywood movies were always dancing around soaking wet.

"The water symbolizes female sexual fulfillment," he'd stuttered.

Oh, what the hell. I dipped my hand into the rill and flicked more water on my shoulders, my face. I had left Albéniz and Tárrega behind and now composed my own joyous finale filled with glissandos and trills. I whispered a thank you to my husband for his maddening plucking, threw myself into the musicality of my own Granada, my own memories of the Alhambra, and continued to rise.

Federico García Lorca

FUENTE VAQUEROS

Thanasis Maskaleris

(Written after my visit to Federico García Lorca's village—long ago.)

¡Oh pueblo perdido, en la Andalucia del llanto!
—Federico García Lorca

We left Granada with invalid senses.
The Moorish splendors had exhausted us—
the unbearable serenity of the courtyards and gardens
where the sensual and the metaphysical lived in one breath,
attuned to the music of architecture and the ceaseless murmur
   of water:
Time and Passion gnawing at one another
under the bursting pomegranate suns.

The flowering tombs of Albaicín had wounded us—
the maddening fragrance of lemon trees
mingled with the ancient stench of sunless alleys,
the starving cats-cursed souls of Moorish lovers—
on perennial watch in the shadow of the Alhambra.

145

We set out...
The interurban trundled across the fertile plain,
slowly like a journey of memory.
Never have I seen so many streams! Flooding mud streams twisting
through ploughed fields and reeds and poplar trees.

"Fuente Vaqueros!
We came to the village square.
Aimless dogs and empty balconies stared at us.
A small puzzled chorus led the way to Lorca's house.
His street lay covered with black muck
kneaded by oxen and the Civil Guard.
The house of his childhood humble and lifeless—
withering flowers on the balcony,
strings of pimientos streaming from the ceiling
down to the burning hair of the girl
that froze in a dream with her elbows on the window sill.

Walking back toward the square
we saw a blacksmith driving nails through the heart of Spain.
His old uncle came to greet us:
"Ay, Federico ... "
Shy, Moorish-eyed children encircled us.
My little son Dionysos took a toy mouse from his magic pocket
and set it in motion after them ...They scurried off, but quickly
    turned back and laughed in gusts ...

And then Lorca came ...
From the dark-green branches he looked on,
and his sombre face trembled with bitter joy
as he saw little Dionysos with his spontaneous theatre
amusing the abandoned children of Spain.

The Author's New Dress

¡OLE!

MJ Pramik

When putting on a new dress really changes things.

"*Golpe! Golpe!*" demanded Virginia. "Shoulders back. Where is your head? *Marcando!*"

I began taking flamenco lessons as an experiment prior to my first trip to Spain. It was a *Why not?* endeavor, my trial-by-fire defiance of genetics, an attempt to transform my curvy Polish body and sensible personality into that of a vibrant and charismatic *bailarina*. I'd read that it takes three weeks of practice to effect a change in habit, so I decided to try a seven-week flamenco class prior to my week-long stay in Seville, my ultimate goal: to find the perfectly fitted shoes and svelte flamenco-*Semana Santa*-Feria-dress, thus achieving a massive metamorphosis. Why not dare to buck the odds?

Finding my San Francisco Bay Area class on the first day of my enrollment really tested my determination to study flamenco. Lines Dance Studio, host of Virginia Iglesias's Flamenco Academy of Dance, had moved from the location I'd visited to retrieve my ballerina daughter two decades before. It was no longer situated comfortably in the heart of the "safe" Civic Center neighborhood of San Francisco.

This I didn't know. I drove around the central plaza several times and finally called.

"Oh, we moved years ago. We're on 7th Street, between Market and Mission," a velvety male voice crooned.

Zigzagging across Market Street, I realized the new location was in a building on the old skid row—one of the last blocks in San Francisco left untouched by the throngs of recent well-heeled transplants, likely due to the busy Social Security Administration building down the block and the sizeable heroin treatment center around the corner. Saturday at noon the street people slept in, and I wove through them as I hurried from my parked car to the sanctuary of an ancient brick building. The stair access was on lockdown; the only way up was an ancient elevator manned by a heavily tattooed millennial listening to tunes wafting from a crackly battery-powered radio.

Master teacher Virginia Iglesias possesses the patience of Job. For the past thirty years she has lived life rooted in her Spanish heritage, dedicating herself solely to the art of flamenco. Her website touts her extensive training at the most renowned flamenco academies in Madrid, where she began her professional dance career. She's choreographed for and performed with Spanish dance companies and toured internationally. Even today, she lives in Spain part of the year, a wise professorial choice for this wholly Spanish art form, I thought.

A gorgeous redhead of a mysteriously becoming age, Virginia held her head high and straight. Her posture oozed "professional dancer." Her bold printed skirt and turquoise flamenco shoes underscored her prowess. In the cavernous studio with long windows abutting the soaring ceiling, she was accompanied by Jorge Liceaga, musical director, *cantaor* and guitarist. Jorge hailed from Mexico City, and, like Virginia, has performed internationally for decades.

"Look in that closet; take this." Virginia handed me the key for the short wooden door in a pale green wall. Assorted flamenco shoes tumbled out. I scrounged for a matching pair, two well-worn, pinching Capezios. They'd do for my first lessons. I was taken aback by the tiny nails studding the toes and heels. So that's how they made all that noise!

Flamenco calls for strong hamstrings and elegant arms, neither of which I possess. Facing the front mirror, I stood in stark contrast with the poised style of my classmates, all women save one middle-aged man. They clearly knew the routine; I imitated to the best of my modest abilities.

"The more you practice, the stronger your hamstrings become," Virginia promised.

"*Planta, planta.*"

"*Planta*-ing" one's foot is achieved by striking the ball onto the floor. A twinge of pain developed after only a few minutes. Slinking to the back of the room, I followed those before me. We repeated and reviewed each choreographic set. Jorge strummed the Spanish guitar as we students stomped across the worn wooden second floor of the 107-year-old building.

"*Palmas, palmas.*"

Hands clapped *sordas*—muffled pops made by cupped hands—or *secas*—strong, dry strikes. In theory, the *palmas* are syncopated with the rhythms of the music and the feet. But I've never been able to walk, pat my head, and rub my belly at the same time, so for each hour-long class I felt like a klutz.

"Focus only on the feet—just the feet. You can add the hands and arms later." Virginia peered straight ahead into the floor-length mirror and met my eyes from where I hid in the back row.

After the first class, and each one thereafter, I applied ice to my knees, then popped two ibuprofen. My knee brace did not add grace to my form. With steely determination, I arrived on time for every single lesson prior to my departure for Seville. *Ouch!* I did accomplish an authentic finger motion, which Virginia complimented, but the heel-drop *tacón* escaped me.

Flamenco has its roots in the music of the Romani people who lived in the Punjab region of Northeast India, migrating westward circa 1,000 BCE. Flamenco's rapid-fire foot movements are reminiscent of the stomping ankle-belled *kathak* dance form from northern Asia. Indian emigrations spread west over several hundreds of years, bleeding into the Balkans, Germany and France. Upon their arrival in northeastern Spain (near Barcelona) around the fifteenth century, these clans met with tribes who migrated out of Egypt, crossed the Straits of Gibraltar, and settled in Andalusia. These southern wanderers became known as *gitanos*—from the Spanish *egiptanos* or Egyptians—today's gypsies. Often persecuted and forced to move, these vagabonds were suspect to townspeople. Their plaintive song, *gitano*, decried their misery and misfortune. Usually sung by a single male, *gitano* comes out rough and raw. Only later, in the nineteenth century, did they don their boots and reaffirm this injustice in their fierce, hammering dance. Castanets entered the flamenco lexicon in the 1900s, as a tourist attraction.

Triana, the middle-class neighborhood across the Guadalquivir River from the posh tourist center of Seville, housed the gypsy tribes for centuries. In her excellent book, *A Cultural Journey Through Andalusia: from Granada to Seville*, Gwynne Edwards documents in detail the fascinating evolution of flamenco. My own initial experience with this history arrived when I wandered through Triana alone in the evening on my third night in Seville and heard a *siguirya (cante grande)*, the saddest and darkest of gypsy songs, wafting from the window of a café. The intensity and heartbreaking tone reminded me of the *siguirya* described by Edwards:

> *Cuando yo me muera,*   When I come to die.
> *Te pio un encargo,*   I ask of you one favor,
> *que con las trenzas de*   that with the braids of
> *tu pelo negro*   your black hair
> *me marren las manos.*   they tie my hands.

A visit to the Museum of Flamenco Dance welcomed me into the world of flamenco in a different way than my feeble attempts at *golpé* and *palmas* did. Historical presentations of the flamenco greats, frayed costumes rescued from several hundred years of dance, and videos of the specific strains of dance further opened this realm to me. That evening I watched four performers of classical flamenco at Casa Del Flamenco in the Barrio de Santa Cruz, also known as the Juderia, the former Jewish Quarter. On the stage, a large, square, raised-wooden structure and four colorful chairs sat across from the audience seated around three sides. The Andalusian tiles adorning the walls provided a richly textured background for the female dancer, in white blouse and a polka-dotted flounce skirt like those I'd already seen in many shops. Her three male counterparts dressed in black. Her tall handsome partner in the *Sevillanas*—the light and lively social dancing enjoyed at Seville's April *Feria* and weddings—added a black jacket.

I decided to return for a second performance two evenings later, which proved more intense and captivating. All performers, mostly attired in black, channeled the gypsy angst and isolation. The male singer in particular gave voice to their pain as his high-pitched yet deep-throated wail plunged those seated around him into the anguish of their existence. The last *cante chico* dance between a woman and young man did allow some joy, *alegría,* to creep back onto the dark stage. Their footwork blazed across the polished floor.

Wandering home that night from the nearby Catedral de Santa María de la Sede and window-shopping in the dark, I spied the perfect flamenco dress. *My colors.* I'd always known the classic red-and-black polka-dotted standards didn't fit my personality, but I didn't know what I sought until that moment. This *Semana Santa/Feria* dress oozed sexiness in apricot, turquoise and deep blue. In that shop window, even the headless mannequin wore it well. This was *my* dress. Next to the mannequin hung a floor-to-ceiling photograph of a fetching dark-haired young woman in profile, her hoop earring large and luscious. The shop name: Lina.

After returning to Hotel Casa Imperial, I traced the shop via smartphone with the aid of my techie roommate, Tania: Calle Lineros, numero 17. I'm GPS-challenged, and Seville is far from a grid with a readable map. I had to ask for Calle Linares every five minutes, but I eventually rediscovered the shop on my own. The dress, in all its glory, still graced the front window. It being the week before *Semana Santa*, the shopkeepers calmly helped a steady stream of customers. After a short wait, I was able to beckon over a young woman and ask the price of the dress. Replying in Spanish, she showed me the tag. *Half of my April rent. Of course.* In addition, the hand-sewn mélange of colors and ruffles was meant for a much slimmer, taller woman. I reasoned with myself to do the sensible thing and walk straight out of the store. But before I left, I decided I needed to try it on … just once.

As I stood in front of the mirror hardly breathing, my mother's dictum crept into my mind: *You can't make a silk purse out of a sow's ear.* What my mother didn't know was that this feat of farfetched ambition had actually been accomplished in 1921. A team of creative scientists from MIT conducted an experiment to create "silk" from pork byproducts. *Sevillanos*, and all Spaniards, should appreciate this bizarre triumph, overloaded as their diet is with every form of pork imaginable—ham, prosciutto, bacon, and assorted "luncheon meats."

The MIT researchers had simply decided to do something everyone said was impossible, much like my decision to become a flamenco dancer, slither into a slimming dress, and shout *olé!* The laboratory masters reduced over one hundred pounds of sows' ears—I kid you not; their raw material garnered a certification from Wilson and Co., a Chicago meatpacker who supplied the ears—to ten pounds of glue. Trial and error led them to devising a means to create strands of "silk" from the glue by imitating the silkworms' process. They spun these strands into cloth from which two silk purses were created in medieval designs. These wildly motivated academics hadn't given up. Neither would I.

"I'll take the dress."

The blond salesperson, in elegant pantsuit and patterned silk scarf, read me the price again to make sure I'd heard her correctly.

"*Si, si.*" I stood in a trance.

The seamstress was summoned. Rocío Montero descended the stairs with a regal carriage; she was the older sister of the elegant blond, Mila. I liked her immediately. She spoke little English, and I spoke less Spanish. She wore sensible working-woman shoes and the requisite colorful scarf. And glasses. Like I do.

"No worry, no worry. We fix it. Will fit." She smiled, quickly ripped out the stitches in all seams and began to pin and pin. In less than ten minutes she'd collected all my dimensions, the same kind of red tomato pincushion my mother had worn for years wrapped around her left wrist.

The sisters nodded together, smiling at me as I drooped in the bedraggled layers of crinoline. The voluminous garment weighed down my shoulders. As I stood there, wilting, beginning to waver in my commitment, I noticed a photograph on the back of the atelier:

a wall-length black and white portrait of Princess Grace of Monaco descending a staircase on the arm of Prince Rainier. Smiling broadly, she wore a white *Semana* dress, all ruffles and eyeleted lace. I caught Rocío's eye and gestured to the picture.

"*Sí*, our mother made the dress for her."

I was certainly in capable hands.

Two days later I hurried back to Lina's at seven o'clock after a long day of travels outside the city. The sisters had stayed open late for me. Much to my shock, the dress did not fit—too low cut up front, too long, too baggy.

I was heartbroken, but Rocío smiled reassuringly. "No worry, no worry."

She pinned and tucked yet again. I would leave Seville in a day and a half, no time for another fitting. We negotiated that they would ship the dress to San Francisco, keeping our fingers crossed. As a parting gift, Rocío presented me with a pair of red crystal earrings surrounded by stones the color of the ruffles on my dress.

The dress appeared at the front door of my San Francisco flat eight days later. The magnificent turquoise-coral-green-deep-blue silk flounces and circular cuffs were nestled in a large box of tulle-like tissue. I held my breath in anticipation ... and of course, it fit perfectly. I sighed with relief and a deep sense of fulfillment. Who said I couldn't become a silk purse?

Flamenco Dancer

FINDING MY INNER GYPSY

Laurie McAndish King

When I was a little girl, I wanted to be a gypsy. Gypsies got to travel anywhere in the world. They lived in wagons that looked like fancy playhouses with big wooden wheels and bright curtains and lanterns that glowed at night. Gypsies knew how to play guitar, danced like firestorms and could foretell the future. The women wore red dresses and sparkly gold hoop earrings. Some of them even had gold teeth!

All that I knew for certain, but there were other things I suspected. I was pretty sure gypsies didn't have to do any work, besides chopping firewood and hunting rabbits to eat. Also, they seemed to have a special status that exempted them from having to abide by laws, which some regular adults resented, probably because they were crabby and narrow-minded from spending way too much time at office jobs. Gypsies were free.

I wanted to run away with the gypsies. I was sure they would take me; they had a reputation for that. I would *become* a gypsy, piercing my ears and making my living telling fortunes. We would travel the world together, eating campfire food and dancing until dawn. These fantasies swirled in my eight-year-old mind as I danced on our front porch wearing my favorite skirt, the red one with three layers of ruffles, hoping some gypsies would drive by.

As I prepared to visit Andalusia many years later—after spending way too much time, myself, at office jobs—my early gypsy fantasies returned. Andalusia was the crossroads of cultures for centuries and the birthplace of flamenco, which was later adopted by gypsies. The region might give me a glimpse of the culture that had inhabited my childhood imagination and inspired my love of travel. But now my fantasies were juxtaposed with disturbing things I'd heard about gypsies in the intervening years.

A TV documentary had shown them scamming residents of Los Angeles by installing poor quality asphalt and roofing, then disappearing before their customers could complain—and before lawyers could retaliate. Gypsies apparently lied and thieved. Not only that, they also hoarded gold and married off their girls at far too young an age. What sort of gypsy would I find in Andalusia?

I arrived during *Semana Santa*—Holy Week, the week before Easter—which turned out to be a perfect time to visit. The city of Seville was alive with preparations and celebrations by the members of *hermandades*, or religious brotherhoods, which have celebrated *Semana Santa* for centuries with processions of elaborate floats. My first stop was at the gypsy church, the Iglesia del Cristo de los Gitanos de Sevilla. Its brotherhood, the Réal, Ilustre y Fervorosa Hermandad Sacramental, Ánimas Benditas y Cofradía de Nazarenos de Nuestro Padre Jesús de la Salud y María Santísima de las Angustias Coronada —also known as the Hermandad de los Gitanos, or Brotherhood of the Gypsies—was established in 1753.

No one at the church wore red. I saw no gold teeth, either. The people there looked just like everyone else in Seville. Some of my other preconceived notions were mistaken, too. I'd thought that perhaps a gypsy brotherhood would be poor—all that travel had to be expensive, and how much wealth can roofers and rabbit hunters amass, anyway?

But the Hermandad de los Gitanos' gorgeous floats, or *pasos*, told another story. Elephant-sized exaltations of intricately worked gold and silver—some as delicate as the finest lace—literally held tons of precious metals. How had the gypsies accumulated all this wealth? Did they steal it? I felt guilty just imagining such behavior.

In recent times, financial support came from the late María del Rosario Cayetana Alfonsa Victoria Eugenia Francisca Fitz-James-Stuart y de Silva, the 18th Duchess of Alba. The Duchess was not a gypsy herself, but she clearly shared their free-spirited approach to life, and her tomb was in the gypsy church.

A billionaire several times over—until a few years ago, when she distributed her wealth to heirs in an attempt to placate them ahead of her marriage, at eighty-five, to a civil servant twenty-five years her junior—the Duchess held forty-nine inherited titles (a Guinness record; she was the senior illegitimate descendant of King James II of England, and the most titled aristocrat in the world). The Duchess was well known throughout Europe for her eccentric habits and appearance—she was inducted into *Vanity Fair*'s International Best-Dressed List Hall of Fame in 2011—and was a darling of gossip magazines until her death in 2014. Her main home was a sprawling palace just a few blocks from the Hermandad de los Gitanos, and she had been quite fond of the brotherhood, providing significant gifts and financial infusions for many years.

My next stop was Triana, the gypsy quarter of Seville and historic home to painters, potters, bullfighters and other poor-yet-noble inhabitants—including the gypsy Carmen, perhaps the most celebrated opera character of all time. Carmen haunts Triana's twisting lanes, still pouting behind mysterious latticed windows or strolling beneath fragrant-blossomed orange trees. It is a district of artists and lovers, secrets and seduction, pain and passion.

The best place to find gypsy passion today, I decided, was in flamenco, which had danced right out of the Triana district into the world. I was inspired to attend a flamenco dance class at the Cristina Hoyas Flamenco Dance Museum. Perhaps I could at least learn the arm movements; they seemed simple enough.

As it turned out, nothing about flamenco is simple. It requires an excellent sense of rhythm, which I will never possess. Once the rhythm is established—"stomp-clap-clap-clap" is the most straight-forward of many variations—one learns the walk, and then the arm movements. Next come the wrist movements (twisting from the inside out, and then the reverse) and then the finger movements ... and then the hip swaying ... and then the shoulder shimmy.

These seven basic movements are combined, by those who can do so, into a fiery, fast-paced dance, emotional and expressive. But for me, it was hopeless. True, I had become a traveler like the gypsies were, but I was neither rich nor free, neither fiery nor passionate in the way they were. I had no hoards of gold, nor red roses between my teeth. I wondered why they'd had a hold on me all these years, and why I felt as though I somehow belonged to the gypsy tribe.

I moved from my hobbled attempts at flamenco to seeing a live performance at one of Seville's finest venues. The sharp, rhythmic clapping alone pulled me in and started my shoulders shimmying. The plaintive song in a minor key, strange yet familiar, tugged at my heart. The dancer's wide, elegant arm movements changed my own posture, opening up a chakra or two, I'm sure. And her sassy hip-swaying, foot-stamping, skirt-wagging sashays completely undid me. This was unlike anything I had experienced.

And finally, I understood—flamenco is not just music and dance. It is percussion and passion, love and longing, hunger and anger. It is all things gypsy—temptation, seduction, defiance. And it is *duende*, that soulful state of evocation, of dark genius, of sorrow's deathly beauty.

Growing up in the midwest in the 1960s, in a Protestant— specifically, Methodist—culture, I was taught to hide my emotions. No one cared much about *feeling*, and certainly not about "negative" feelings—those were never to be aired in public, or even indulged in private.

But the gypsies got it. More than a balance of dark and light, the gypsies' *duende* is a synthesis, a proof that darkness is not only legitimate, but also necessary. It is what my childhood self knew but my adult self had to learn. More than the gypsies' colorful reds and golds, their music and dance, their travels around the world, it was *deunde* —that impenetrable emotion that is beyond conversation—that drew me to the gypsies.

In Seville I had discovered Carmen's legacy. It pervades the city, from spirited flamenco performances to the Callejón del Agua where Carmen used to dance, from the old tobacco factory where she worked to the bullring where she was stabbed to death. It stirred in me a kind of passion that was far from my midwestern roots. And yet, in some mysterious way, that gypsy spirit brought me home.

Woman with Castanets

OF CHESTNUT TREES AND CASTANETS

Antoinette Constable

A friend recently gave me some castanets. Suddenly, I was a child again with a brown, shiny pair, which, in spite of repeated attempts, I never managed to play correctly, though I loved them. Then, as I was about to go to Spain, it occurred to me that many Americans might not even know what they are.

Drifting into sleep, I fell into a sort of reverie, with this question on my lips, ready to ask my fellow residents of the Bay Area, "What are castanets anyway?"

A bearded UCSF student I met at BART answered first. "They are parasites from South Africa, almost undetectable. Symptoms include severe depression, dizziness and a craving for nuts. I know; my brother went to Capetown and suffers from this."

Then the mother of twin babies in a Safeway parking lot chimed in. "It's the latest form of punishment in Russia," she explained with a sigh. "You can tell, because net or *nyet* means forbidden in Russian. Prisoners are beaten with rods, and they don't get any food."

Later, imagining myself at the movies, a Parisian chemist, ahead of me in line, added: "The natural compounds of these mushrooms are highly poisonous and too complex to explain here. But you should be aware that the Borgias fed them to their enemies mixed in wine or H_2O in sauces with horrifying results."

Then, on a Muni train, a hippie-looking fellow from Canada, a photographer, blew smoke rings and offered this nugget: "Castanets are the chips of the largest diamond in the world. They are kept in a secret vault of the Vatican so no one has seen them for 113 years."

Closer to home, I encountered a bare-chested young man washing his car on the street who declared: "Never heard of them. Lived here all my life, and I know all the neighbors. They sure don't live on my street."

Finally, I met Tyrone, an impish boy about seven, in line at the drugstore. I needed something for a headache, caused by the clicking sound in my head. I posed my question to his mother, but the boy answered before she could speak. "They're tap dancing things for your hands," he said, "clackers."

The right answer at last! The noise in my head began to taper down, and I woke up, energized from my sleep, remembering more information about castanets. For one thing, they are shaped like bivalves, the two parts kept close by a loose string you wrap around your thumbs, the curved sides to be held in your palms by your fingers. But most important, they are made of *castan*, the Spanish word for chestnut.

Heading to Spain, I knew that, sadly, not only were chestnut trees hard to find, but so were castanets, born of chestnut wood. In fact, these days chestnut trees make their most common appearance in castanets. They were also once ubiquitous in France, where I grew up.

In the Alps, my family owned a large property with a sweet chestnut grove. The ground was always damp and mossy underfoot in a forest that produced a scented green shade under which we danced wildly as only children can, once we'd removed the prickly shells of chestnuts. The trees generously shed pollen for the bees and endless whitish flowers. Later, after a frantic gathering of sweet chestnuts we roasted them at the far end of the forest inside our favorite chestnut tree, alive though hollowed one fall by thunder. The conkers fell pale green and round on the moss where their soft prickles soon hardened into yellow nails. The nuts glossy as chocolate showed in late summer through cracked-open coverings, three or four to a prickly shell. Once roasted, we peeled away their burning hot casings, inhaled the smoke, munched, wiping blackened fingers on our shorts, under a thick canopy of oval leaves arranged like wide stretched-out fingers caressing the breeze.

Chestnut trees also provided a sweet flour used instead of unavailable wheat flour by the Protestants—hated by the Catholics. The Protestants had taken refuge in the Cevennes part of France, where they chose to live in a land too poor for agriculture. There, they hoped to avoid persecution, arrest and death at the hands of the dragoons of the Catholic king of France. With the chestnut flour, they made porridge and a kind of flat bread, sometimes their only sustenance.

Chestnuts also gave us *Confiture de Chateignes* and *Marrons Glacés*, the first a great spread throughout the year, spooned over toast, nestled into whipped cream or yogurt; the second, a New Year treat when it appeared wrapped in swirls of gold foil oozing with velvety flavor.

I mourn the stately chestnut trees of so many forests and gardens, in addition to their dense shade. Throughout Europe these magnificent trees have vanished, victim like so many other species, of overuse and disease. They gave us many things, castanets, of course, but also their wood, which was prized in construction, especially in roofing, because its spider-repelling qualities, safe storage of artifacts, particularly in castles and museum attics. The loss of these trees in Europe is so severe that China is beginning to manufacture castanets out of fiberglass, which is cheaper, and perhaps very good, *but certainly not the historically real thing*. On the other hand, American scientists are growing virus-resistant chestnut trees so that perhaps the French will one day enjoy more *Confiture de Marrons* and *Marrons Glacés*, while the rest of the world witnesses the resurrection of chestnut wood castanets.

In Seville, I watched a flamenco dancer perform with "clackers" held in her hands high above her head. She became a mesmerizing, swirling column of water, offering and withdrawing herself many times like a rejecting multicolor temptress, displaying herself according to the increasing rhythm of the castanets, the gems from the chestnut tree— not diamonds, perhaps, as that Canadian claimed, but surely just as precious.

Pedro Ximenez Sherry

CONFESSIONS OF A SECRET SHERRY SIPPER

Donna Hemilla

Three sips into my *Alfonso oloroso seco,* the truth hits me: This is not my grandmother's sherry. What I am savoring in the bar down the street from my hotel in Seville tastes nothing like any beverage I've ever consumed. Unlike its more sedate cream sherry relative, this Spanish cousin breathes fire and sensuality. It dances on the tongue and spreads a subtle warmth through the veins. A fourth sip, and I am imagining Antonio Banderas rather than my portly, gravel-voiced waiter, pouring my wine.

By the time I savor the last drop in my glass, a new viticulture obsession takes hold. Silently, I swear a vow to learn—and drink— all I can of this sublime Andalusian nectar and to do my part to change its image.

In most circles, sherry invokes visions of gray-haired grannies, collectors of doilies and porcelain kitties, delicately imbibing from fairy-sized goblets while watching *Masterpiece Theater* on a Sunday night.

On a Sunday night in Andalusia, however, sherry conjures quite another scene. Hoards of young people in jeans and T-shirts crowd the taverns alongside elderly couples still attired in their suits and church dresses. The lines at the bars are deep, the conversations firecracker loud, and the sherry generously poured. Unlike me, no one is ashamed to admit they drink sherry because it is simply a way of life.

Like the stamping of flamenco dancers and the heartbreaking wail of gypsy singers, sherry flows deep in the Andalusian culture. To drink it in Seville, the city that gave the world Carmen, Don Juan, and the famous "Barber," is a richly layered experience—one that I think could at last propel my forbidden sherry love into the light.

You see, before travelling to Seville, I was not a sherry virgin. I first developed a taste for it during a visit to a California B&B where the two retired-schoolteacher owners furnished each room with a cruet of cream sherry and two adorably tiny glasses. One swallow of the honey-sweet, dark amber liquid, and I was hooked. I began making nightly raids on the sherry bottle kept next to the collection of tiny teacups in the B&B's china cabinet.

Several of my own bottles later, I had to admit that I, like the retired schoolteachers, was a sherry sipper. This is not something I tell my friends. To disclose that I fancy a nip of *sherry* in the evenings is an unnecessary admission of growing old, akin to wearing support hose or letting one's roots go gray. Why broadcast the obvious?

That was my old way of thinking before Andalusia.

Now, I imagine myself back home, pouring my wine-snob friends princely glasses of authentic Spanish sherry. "It's what all the hipsters in Spain are drinking," I will tell them. "Notice the crispness, the engaging notes of raisin, the hints of earthy chocolate. *Muy bueno, si?*" However, before I can pour sherry with such authority, I must educate myself. What better place to start than the oldest bar in Spain?

El Reconcillo has been serving food and drink in the heart of Seville since the 1800s. The property itself dates to 1670, hence the claim to being the country's oldest tavern.

Approaching its doors on a Sunday evening, my fellow traveler

Gayle and I find the place a bit intimidating. People spill into the surrounding streets, shouting conversation and clinking glasses. Bravely, we squeeze sideways through the raucous crowd. An imposing L-shaped wooden bar dominates the establishment, its top scarred from centuries of glasses hoisted and drained beneath a curtain of ham haunches dangling from the beamed ceiling. Next to the kitchen, small images of female Catholic saints cover the glass doors of a wooden cabinet.

For not the first time, I marvel at the way Seville's passion for food, drink and all manner of earthly delights exists side by side with intense religious devotion. It's not unusual to see graphic portraits of a suffering Christ sharing cafe wall space with beer advertisements.

We seat ourselves at a table tucked into a back corner and order *salmorejo*, the rich, vibrant-orange Andalusian version of gazpacho, and a salad with smoked salmon. I ask the waiter for his recommendation of a sherry, and he delivers two glasses of an icy cold wine, dry, crisp and white like a chardonnay or pinot grigio. I thought all sherry came in shades of amber. Foolish me. Like a good lover, sherry is full of surprises.

I want to ask the waiter more about this white fino sherry, but he is running full speed to serve a large family party in the back dining room.

On the way back to our hotel, we stop at another tavern where I confess my sherry ignorance to the bartender. He pours me two small tastes.

"Sweet and sweeter," he says, pointing to each glass.

I sip both and decide on sweet. When it comes time to settle our tab, we are astounded to find each of our drinks cost a measly 1.80 Euro. Yes, intoxication in Andalusia comes cheap.

The next day in a cafe on Plaza de la Alfalfa, I find La Gitana manzanilla on tap, a perfect accompaniment to the garlic shrimp tapa

I order. At least I think it is, since it's white and dry. Unfortunately, although I am enjoying sherry sampling, I fear that barhopping is doing little to advance my sherry education.

I must make The Pilgrimage.

Jerez de la Frontera, the birthplace of sherry, lies a pleasant one-hour train ride south of Seville. Since the time of the Phoenicians, around 1100 BCE, this region has produced sherry. Jerez, Sanlúcar de Barrameda and El Puerto de Santa María are the three towns that delineate the famous Sherry Triangle, where 17,000 acres of grapes are under cultivation.

Sir Francis Drake, that privateering British swashbuckler, is credited with popularizing sherry in his homeland after he stole 3,000 casks during the sacking of the coastal town of Cádiz. The U.K. is still sherry's biggest export market.

When I get off the morning train in Jerez, I find a city gleaming with white plastered buildings, red roofs, wide palm-tree-lined streets and a profusion of sherry bodegas. I take a taxi to Bodega Sandeman, which I had read offers the most erudite tours.

When the bodega gates open, I enter the visitor center, a cavernous, softly lit building crammed with rows of pyramid-stacked wine barrels. The bodega's website advertised an English-language tour at 10:30 a.m. It failed to mention, however, that a minimum of two people is required for a tour. As I am the only person here, I feel the sherry knowledge I've come to acquire sliding out of reach. I whine and beg, explaining that I've come all the way from Seville on the train.

The young woman I've been pleading with for admittance disappears into a side room and returns with a young man named Gonzalo, who consents to give me a private tour. I ask him if he's familiar with sherry's reputation in the United States as a drink for old people.

"Ahh, the grannies!" He laughs. "That has to change. We are working on it."

I ask Gonzalo to teach me how sherry is made. We start with the grapes. To be called sherry, a wine can only contain three varieties, and they are all white: muscatel, palomino and Pedro Ximénez, affectionately know in sherry circles as PX. After harvest, grapes are pressed and the juice fermented and then fortified with natural grape alcohol. The yeasts from the fermentation process produce something called flor, a whitish film that settles on top of the wine, preventing it from coming in contact with oxygen. The cellar master decides which wines will continue to age biologically under flor into finos and manzanillas, and which will be allowed to oxidize and darken in color, into olorosos. From there is gets complicated, because sometimes sherry has a mind of its own. Wine that started out as fino or manzanilla can jump ship into the oxidative aging process if their flor dies off. Or the cellar master can fortify the wine with more alcohol to deliberately kill the flor. The death of flor produces amontillado and palo cortado sherries. The naturally sweet moscatel and PX sherries, named after their grape varieties, both age with oxidation. The PX grapes, and sometimes also the moscatel, are sun-dried before pressing, to concentrate the sugar and coloring. The cream sherries are produced by blending varieties.

I follow Gonzalo to a back corner of the bodega to learn about the next production stages. Immediately, I'm overtaken with the heavy scent of overripe grapes, like I'm walking in a vineyard during harvest. I inhale and let out an appreciative sigh.

"We call that the angel's share." Gonzalo smiles. A certain amount of sherry evaporates during the aging process. Its scent hangs on the air the way a woman's seductive perfume lingers after she's left the room. While I'm inhaling, Gonzalo turns classroom-serious.

"You will never understand sherry, if you do not learn what I am about to show you," he announces as he pulls a curtain aside with a flourish. I tingle with both excitement and fear that I will somehow disappoint my young guide if I do not absorb the knowledge he is about to impart.

Behind the curtain, he reveals the *solera* system, the aging process that separates sherry from other wines. The American oak barrels in this room are stacked in four rows, each holding sherry of a different age.

"The top barrels, we call *criaderas*. It means in English something like 'raising up,' like you raise a child."

The bottom row of barrels, he explains, holds the oldest sherry, the solera. From these barrels the sherry is drawn off for bottling. But none of the barrels are ever fully emptied. Two-thirds of the sherry stays behind to mingle with the wine that will be pulled from the row of barrels above it. The process is repeated for each row until the wine missing from the topmost row is replaced with the bodega's latest vintage.

The wine spends at least three years traveling from row to row. Some of the barrels I'm looking at date from 1894, so technically a bottle filled from those could hold wine more than 120 years old. I am in awe over this delicate nurturing process, on one hand, so scientific, and on the other, so dependent upon tradition and human instinct.

As my tour draws to an end, I do feel wiser and more prepared to enjoy the grand finale—a premium sherry tasting. I almost squeal out loud at the sight of the four generous glasses of sherry set out on a plank table, along with bowls of green olives and potato chips.

Since it's barely noon, I have to ask, "What is the proper time of day to drink sherry? In America, we drink it as either an aperitif or an after-dinner dessert wine." Gonzalo raises an eyebrow.

"You can find a time to drink sherry any time of day," he says. "It depends on the sherry."

First, I sip a rare fino, followed by a dry amontillado from the 1894 solera, an olloroso, and, finally, a rich chocolaty PX, both aged more than twenty years. I begin to feel a bit tipsy. California chardonnay has an alcohol content of between 13.5 and 14.5 percent. The alcohol content of the sherry I am drinking ranges from 15 to 20 percent. But I'm not about to leave sherry this luscious on the table. I drink every drop, bid farewell to Gonzalo, and head to the train station on foot to see more of the town.

I get lost. But it's the good kind of lost. I see the sights, meet some construction workers, and hold puzzling conversations in my limited Spanish. I ask a woman on a bicycle for directions. She rides along beside me to make sure I get where I want to go. It must be the sherry that renders Jerez's citizens so mellow.

Since I've returned home, my sherry obsession shows no sign of ebbing. Recently, I visited a Spanish grocery in Berkeley. As my eyes feasted on the rows of finos, manzanillas and amontillados in its wine section, a clerk approached.

"We recommend these for people just being introduced to sherry," he said directing me to the cream sherry shelf.

I'm hardly an expert, but I did harvest some knowledge during the days I spent in Andalusia. It's like when the optometrist flips the lens to a stronger prescription and the bottom line on the eye chart miraculously comes into focus: I now know what I'm looking at when I pick up a bottle of sherry.

Ignoring the clerk's recommendation, instinctively I reach for a respectable fourteen-year-old oloroso, my sherry soul mate. Then I rush home for another imaginary date with Señor Banderas and a large bowl of green olives. And yes, Gonzalo was right: I can find time to drink sherry any time. And I do.

Andalusian Flamingos

I Say Flamenco
And You Say Flamingo

Linda Watanabe McFerrin

Flamenco; it's *flamenco*, not flamingo," I kept telling friends who referred to the wailing, strumming, foot-stomping, finger-snapping, hand-clapping art form that originated in Andalusia as "doing the flamingo."

But I was wrong. It really is the "flamingo" if you translate directly. Actually, the word, *flamenco*, means "flame" in Spanish, and is applied both to the fiery gypsy-influenced dance and to the birds. Flamenco or flamingo, I've long been enthralled by the dance and even took a quick lesson at the Museum of Flamenco Dance in Seville when I got to Spain. However, it was the lanky, brightly plumed birds—*los flamencos*—that I wanted to see when I visited in Andalusia.

Flamingos have completely entranced me ever since I was a little girl, when I first came upon them in one of my many picture books. In *Alice in Wonderland*, the flamingos are the mallets in a game of croquet in the Red Queen's garden. Held upside down, long legs in the air, they are used to smack the croquet balls (live hedgehogs) and send them flying.

It is a whimsical image and it stuck. Later, I'd encounter flamingos as lawn decorations (plastic) in front of coastal bungalows and as pool ornaments (actual birds) at various resorts. I did not, however, have an opportunity to see these eerily beautiful creatures in the wild until I came to Andalusia. I'd missed them in Tanzania and in the Camargue in southern France—where my husband, Lawrence, was fortunate enough to sight a few.

I am no birder; I am not dedicated to the serious pursuit, observation and identification of birds around the world. I have, however, sought out and written about some very special avifauna. I also feel blessed to live next to a lake that's right on the Pacific flyway and home to egrets greater and lesser, night herons, pelicans, cormorants, coots, various kinds of geese and ducks and lots and lots of gulls. Although all of these birds captivate me, I don't believe there is another denizen of earth, sky or sea that intrigues me to the same degree as the flamingo. Maybe it's the tiny ruby eyes, the fabulous shrimp-pink feathers or the ultra-skinny, ultra-long black legs. They also happen to manifest an incredibly weird courting behavior. A group of flamingos is actually called a "flamboyance," and in these colorful troupes or "pats" the gregarious birds will execute a courtship dance as formal and as meticulously articulated as a … well … as a beautiful flamenco performance.

In Spain, as in France and only a few other countries around the Mediterranean, flamingos are found in very select locations. One of these is in the wilderness area in North Málaga Province, in a region where most of the land is now devoted to agriculture. Laguna de Fuente de Piedra Nature Reserve is one of Spain's most important wetlands. The lagoon itself—a shallow and highly saline body of water only 4.5 miles long and 1.5 miles wide, that has endured in spite of many attempts by the salt industry to drain it and extract the salt—is the home of slews of bird species. But the star of this particular show is the Greater Flamingo or *Phoenicopterus roseus*. Like the French Camargue, Fuente de Piedra is one of the two most important regular breeding enclaves for these birds in the Mediterranean region and northwestern Africa, and though their numbers vary depending upon rainfall, up to 700,000 birds have been recorded in the colony during breeding years. It is also the only European breeding site for the Lesser Flamingo, *Phoeniconaias minor.*

For this part of our journey, Lawrence, our friend Thanasis and I were staying on the coast midway between Algeciras and Málaga. Fuente de Piedra was miles and miles away, and although I wanted to devote the day to the flamingos, Thanasis had other ideas. He had memories of staying there, on the Costa del Sol, fifty years before, a youthful poet with a toddler son, living in white seaside villages so reminiscent of his native Greece. Marbella, Benalmádena, Torremolinos, we had to visit at least some of his old haunts as we sped eastward, lingering on shores freighted with memories. It was nearly impossible and certainly unkind to drag him away from it all, and I began to fret as morning melted into noon and then early afternoon there on the delirious dream-addled coast. When we finally broke away, shadows were already beginning to lengthen, and I was becoming concerned that we would arrive too late at Fuente de la Piedra.

I needn't have worried. We pulled into the reserve a short while before sunset, in perfect light. As it turns out, the best time to view the flamingos is at the start or the end of the day. Once there, I was immediately transported back to my childhood, feeling a little like Alice in the midst of a very strange wonderland, the late afternoon sunlight flashing on the hot-pink birds as they flew over the lagoon and came to rest in the shallow waters. We wandered the grounds to find the bird blind, Lawrence temporarily distracted by the legions of other wild creatures. I followed a small path, found the blind, and using my camera as my binoculars, filled every frame with flamingos. I could have watched them forever. We stayed until sunset fell in very much the same way as a curtain falls after a beautiful pageant. It was a haunting close to a fabulous natural tableau, one that was curiously soothing and reassuring in whatever direction we turned.

In a few days our sojourn in Andalusia drew to a close, and we toasted our travels—our good times in Ronda, Estepona, Cádiz, Marbella, Torremolinos, Benahavis and Morocco—at a dinner and flamenco performance where my quick lessons in flamenco dance in Seville came in handy. When the principal male dancer in the small troupe began to look about for a partner from the audience, I felt doomed, ducking my head in un-flamenco-like modesty as I tried to avoid eye contact. Naturally, he selected me. And so I took the stage for a mortifying exhibition as I stomped and hand-clapped along for what seemed like forever in dreadful imitation of my professional partner.

That night as I attempted to dance the flamenco, I wasn't thinking about the birds. If I had been, I'm sure my performance would have taken flight. As it was, I was quite flat-footed, though I did flap my arms about and managed to execute a kind of bird-like walk for the audience. Nothing so beautiful as either the gypsies or the birds resting, courting and nesting after their long flight from Africa, although at that moment, Flamenco and flamencos had become one for me.

Indeed I was doing the flamingo!

al-Andaluz, based on the Alhambra's paving patterns,
handmade print by Maryly Snow

EL GALLINERO:
CAPTIVITY IN A CHICKEN COOP

Maryly Snow

For a week I'd been a near-captive in El Gallinero, the chicken coop. I'd signed up to be printmaker-in-residence for a week with master printer Maureen Booth, aided by her husband-driver-editor-photographer-house-manager Mike. They (he American, she British) live in Pinos Genil, a small village of 1,400 people in the foothills of the Sierra Nevada in a hundred-year-old farmhouse twenty minutes outside of Granada. Maureen has hosted printmakers from around the world for nearly fifty years. I would be working with her one-on-one, making a series of solar etching plates from my collages of measuring devices, inspired by Heisenberg's Uncertainty Principle.

Before going, I proudly told friends that I would be staying for a week in a chicken coop making art, which sounded romantic, poetic, and adventuresome. But secretly I worried: I had little Spanish (maybe thirty words tops), no car, no travel companion, and plenty of insecurities about my art making. I also had some images I needed to take to the next stage: Help with platemaking and printing for a week would be useful, and Pinos Genil was not far from Seville. Mike and Maureen had cautioned me that a week was not long enough, but it was all I had.

I knew in advance that "the accommodation does not include meals but it has a cozy, fully-equipped kitchen with a wood-burning stove. There's a selection of restaurants in the village that serve hearty Spanish soul food, a couple of grocery stores, two bakeries and a few tapas bars. Access to supermarkets in Granada is easy, as the return bus stops at our door. Just tell the driver your stop is 'Maureen.'"

I also knew that, upon arrival, there'd be food in my *casita*, but I'd have to buy more for the week. I'd imagined tracing the Rio Genil for an hour into the village for evening meals, bringing a book, listening to Spanish, meeting some locals—and shopping for provisions. I knew I would never walk further, following the river into Granada, because my perpetually sore feet would have had enough standing in the print studio. I wondered whether "my coop" would be a bed and breakfast, a small house of my own, or something in between.

I spotted Mike at the Granada train station right away, his wispy gray hair and ruddy complexion screaming Anglo, not Spanish. I was eager to settle into El Gallinero but Mike and Maureen had other plans, namely lunch. As we drove, Mike explained that El Gallinero had once been Maureen's painting studio, but after she moved her studio closer to the main house, it sheltered chickens. They didn't last long before another room was added onto the first, the structure then cobbled together from a variety of sources: double doors from a nunnery, wood beams from an old house.

From the train station, we drove straight to lunch, to what Mike claimed was "our favorite authentic working-class Granadino bar, not like those high-priced places in Seville that rip you off"—this after my delightful week in Seville where my fellow travelers and I marveled at the delicious and cheap tapas. *Oh dear*, I thought.

We drove to El Bar Molinero in El Zaidín, a nondescript neighborhood of mid-rise apartment blocks in the south of Granada. This itself was a bit of shock after a week in Seville's Centro Historico, but it was in Bar Molinero that I learned "true" Spanish bars are filled with families, children in strollers, old men with canes, dogs on leashes, noisy conversations and televisions, the sort of place where *tapas* come free with a glass of beer or wine, the food to keep you healthy and sober. When tapas are free, they aren't on the menu. All I saw on this menu were *raciones*. How much food comes with a *raciones* anyway?

The Booths were trying hard to be helpful. "How about eggs and poor man's potatoes?" they asked. But I was lost: a week of mouth-watering Sevillian menus left me unprepared for ordering without one. I ate ordinary tapas—potato chips, a two-bite slice of roasted pork on toast, served on a paper plate.

Finally we began our ride to Pinos Genil, twenty minutes up the twisty turns of Carretera Güéjar Sierra, passing small family farms with groves of olive trees, wilder than the neatly topped thousands seen from the train. This is when I asked the first of the several questions that had bedeviled me for weeks: Would I have to cook on a wood-burning stove? No, thank goodness, but it would be my only source of heat.

A sudden turn into a short driveway on the edge of the steep hillside brought us to the Booths: white-washed stone buildings connected by brick paths made uneven by tree roots of bay, cedar, wild olive, chestnut, and pine (*pinos*).

El Gallinero. There it was. Reassuring in its white-washed sturdiness. Mike unhooked the curious bungee cord connecting the front iron gates to the double front doors. Inside, two spacious and well-lighted rooms faced me: a sitting room/bedroom with a library and a long, well-lighted desk, followed by a kitchen, sitting and eating area. The wood-burning stove was supplied with ample olive wood. A small deck overlooked the rugged Rio Genil valley. Comfortable. Nary a hint of chickens. Three cats came bounding in. After happily greeting them, I learned the news: You could let them in, but you would never get them out, as they only obeyed Maureen. The bungee cord prevented the cats from busting in.

Hungry that Friday evening, I had no idea how old the henhouse food was: olive oil for the pasta, no pasta pot; oatmeal, no milk; some fresh fruit, oranges, kiwis hiding under bananas spotted with age. Starved for dinner, and needing food for the week, Mike drove us into Pinos Genil looking for a *tienda* that sold *comestibles*. Since the stores in both Pinos and Cenes de la Vega (the village closer to Granada) were closed, Mike drove us into Granada to Lidl, a German-owned supermarket chain specializing in family packs of food. We ate that night at La Fabrica, a small bar closest to the Booth's house. Same tapas.

In the morning, I walked along the path down the steps to Maureen's printmaking studio nestled under the terrace. Housing two etching presses, flat files, work tables, a gas heater, and flooded with daylight, I could see it was a good work environment.

Time for my next bedeviling question: What did Maureen think of the five film transparencies I'd brought? She examined the films carefully with a loupe, ran her finger over the negative areas, and declared the inkjet films unacceptable: We needed laser. She suggested that after the weekend we take the bus into Granada to visit her favorite *fotocopias* place, the one across from Teatro Isabel la Católica. They would print my digital files as laser transparencies.

In the meantime, I began sketching some of the Alhambra paving patterns that had captured my attention. Pencil in hand, sitting in the warm, sunny studio, I was utterly content, knowing that as soon as I stepped outside the studio, the real world (no Spanish, no car, no map, unexpected cold weather) would impede, would imprison me in Pinos. I transferred the sketched images onto acetate film using thick India ink. On Sunday we exposed the film, creating four small solar plates.

I was eager for our bus trip to Granada. I'd discover the stops, fare, and route, gaining some semblance of independence. But it drizzled that day, and Mike drove us instead. We visited Maureen's spa, a marvel of underwater jets and thundering downspouts that made my recalcitrant muscles relax. Todoncopias, the copy place, adjusted my digital collages, printed them onto laser transparencies. Cost? Less than a Euro each. Eventually these films made excellent solar plates.

Back in El Gallinero it was time to tackle the wifi problem (*wee-fee* in Spanish). Mike called in his computer guy, whose elaborate Bluetooth-weefee-data-roaming work-around quit once he left the premises. So Mike lent me his old PC. All week I grappled with the Spanish keyboard, barely conquering the email @ sign.

The workshop schedule fell into the pattern of Spanish daily life: 9:30 to 2:00, then a three-hour siesta, resuming around 5:00 until 8:00 pm. During siesta, Mike and Maureen ate their largest meal of the day (*almuerzo*), then took a two-hour nap. This was the ideal time for me to shop in the village, exactly when the stores and bar kitchens were closed, making provisioning problematic.

But my main torments were the cold and my tussles with the wood stove. Starting fires every day was fun, but loading the humongous burls was a challenge I usually lost, the heavy olive blobs crashing my existing fire into a smoldering mess of "smoke gets in your eyes," billowing into my two rooms and all my clothes.

Pinos Genil isn't always colder than Granada, but it was that March, one night dropping to 37°F. One sunny, cold Sunday, I wore five layers—undershirt, over-shirt, vest, sweater, jacket—as I walked to the village. There, on the main street, I was stunned to see more than a hundred people eating outdoors, tables lining the sidewalk, crowding the street, diners chatting and laughing, seemingly oblivious to the cold. No wonder Maureen called me a *friolera*, someone sensitive to the cold.

Sometimes Mike visited the printmaking studio, often mentioning that he'd started a new fire. I'd thank him profusely, always uncertain whether this was a special favor or part of his routine, his job. This sort of uncertainty added to my sense of dislocation.

Once I joined Mike and Maureen for *almuerzo*. Mike had cooked *cocido*, a traditional Spanish stew of mixed meats—lamb, beef, ham, chicken, and blood sausage—plus chickpeas, garlic, leeks and potatoes, boiled then simmered on a wood-burning stove. The multiple flavors were rich and complex, the chickpeas crunchy, not mushy.

Another afternoon I walked down the perilous hairpin road determined to find the bus stop and visit Granada's new Centro Federico García Lorca and the nearby *catedral*, two birds with one bus. The breath-taking cathedral was too frigid for the forty-minute audio tour, but outside the streets thronged with people; the air pulsed with drums. I was thrilled to watch a small *Semana Santa* parade march by, hundreds of red pointy hoods (*capirotes*) over purple robes, followed by, a few cobbled streets away, white *capirotes* over maroon robes. The new Lorca Center displayed nothing: it's a performance venue.

Eventually I'd learned about Antonio, the local taxi man, hiring him to drive me up the road to Güéjar Sierra, the gateway to the Sierra Nevada. The sunny central plaza was filled with chatting old men, while on nearby side streets old women sat on benches, and people of all ages talked balcony-to-balcony. In the Plaza Mayor, I gambled on a *tarta al whiskey*. A large wedge of whiskey ice cream pie with traditional Andalusian double mounds of whipped cream, drizzled with burnt caramel sauce, seemed too large to eat in ten minutes, but by the time Antonio arrived, the tarta was gone.

My last evening in Pinos Genil, I asked Mike what he and Maureen were doing for dinner. He suggested going out for a variety of tapas. We returned to El Zaidín and a loud, exuberant, crowded bar. We began with the fish brochette, (succulent ocean white fish, calamari, and barbequed green pepper with salad), followed by the *California*, stuffed pork loin topped with a soft cooked quail egg on the ubiquitous bed of mayo and ketchup. We finished with the eponymous *Romero*, a small toast with a tender artichoke heart crossed by two anchovies on a layer of aioli. When Mike went up to the bar to pay *la cuenta*, there was an awkward moment where roles and expectations were never made explicit. He thought I had invited them out; I thought we would share the price. I understood that after fifty years in Spain, the Booths are thoroughly Spanish: polite, accommodating, and indirect, not like us more candid Yanks. Lesson learned: Pay at the bar.

I also learned why the Booths said one week wasn't enough. It took that long just to learn my way out of a feeling of captivity into my more familiar and fun spirit of exploration both in and out of the studio.

Spanish Paella

COOKING WITH RASHIDA

Lynne Rutan

Metal frames on the counter brace three leathery pig legs, their black hooves still attached. A dark-haired chef, brow furrowed, performs surgery on one of the legs, slicing tissue-thin triangles of meat. He could be cutting diamonds, his concentration is so great; at $75 a pound, the ruby-colored *jamón belloto* he carves is a precious jewel. The slices arrive at our table as a dark rose, petals veined with white fat. They are my first taste of the treasures of Spanish cuisine, served in the venerable El Pimpi Restaurant in Málaga, Spain. Rashida Riedel, for the next four days my cooking teacher and guide in Andalusia's Costa del Sol, begins her culinary instruction.

I've just arrived from the United States and, although punch-drunk with jetlag, excitement at beginning a new adventure buoys me. When a trip to Andalusia set me dreaming about Spanish food and wine, a friend recommended the cooking classes Rashida teaches in her Marbella home overlooking the Mediterranean, both for their taste of Spain and the healthy preparation she advocates. Through Active Gourmet Holidays I signed up with Rashida for cooking lessons in the mornings and afternoon tours of wineries and artist colonies in the Costa del Sol. I raise a slice of the pork delicacy to my lips, eager to begin my studies.

At about 4 p.m., our lunch finished, we wander the maze of walking streets in Málaga's historic quarter. Despite late winter rain and wind, blossoming orange trees fill the plaza of the massive Málaga Cathedral with the sweet scent of approaching spring. I peek in the ornate interior, but nothing, not even a religious experience, can perk me up. It has been twenty-four sleepless hours since I left the United States, and I'm dying to get to my hotel in Marbella. Still, as we walk for what seems like miles, through ancient, twisting alleyways, I begin to recognize some of the storefronts we have passed before.

Rashida's confident footsteps falter; she looks around in confusion. Her body language says it before she does. "I can't find the car park."

I'm too tired to puzzle out why she doesn't know Málaga's old labyrinthine byways. When we finally find the car, I'm in no condition to sightsee and doze through the forty-five-minute drive to crawl into my bed at the Villa Marbella Hotel.

For my first day, I'm refreshed and ready, but before we head to her kitchen Rashida drags me in her wake, trolling Marbella's indoor fish market for ingredients of the meals she'll teach me to cook.

"Your eyes can help tell if the fish is wild and fresh," Rashida instructs, comparing two batches of sea bass. "Look for the darkest black on the fish back and rough scales, and if you want to know, *tell* them 'that fish is farm raised,'" Rashida advises. "If you ask, of course they'll say it's wild."

Provisioned, at last we head to Rashida's kitchen, built in a functional U-shape with long counters and green cabinets. It is decorated with a cheerful garden of flowered ceramic tiles. The space fits her like a long-loved shoe—unpretentious, neither slick nor fashionable, but attractive, comfortable and well-used. On today's menu are: seafood paella, white gazpacho, and almond and mascarpone mousse with strawberry coulis. "I've had a *passion*..." Rashida taps her wooden spoon for emphasis, "a *passion* for cooking since I was very young." In her family home in Algeria, traditional fare that blended the flavors of the Mediterranean, Middle East and Africa was fine for regular meals, but butter and cream, the ingredients of Algeria's French colonizers, were *de rigueur* for company. Even as a pre-teen, she had an instinct for the tenets of healthy cooking. "I was always telling my mother to cook with less cream and more olive oil."

Leaving her Arab and Muslim childhood behind, she touched down in Paris and London, spending the '70s and '80s modeling and partying with her first husband, a wealthy Lebanese, and the international jet set. Now she lives with her second husband, a Dutchman named Ton, in a rambling villa with views of the Rock of Gibraltar and Africa. Cool white marble floors, oriental carpets, and a sunken alcove with latticed wood screens and low banquettes where I catch an afternoon siesta, bring Rashida's Middle Eastern roots into her home.

Donning apron, jeans and sensible shoes, her shoulder-length brown hair clipped in a no-nonsense twist, she tells me she started her cooking classes a decade ago, when "I needed to find something to do because I got too old to go to the clubs."

Rashida and I begin the paella, hovering over her well-burnished two-handled pan as she heats it to cook the rice al dente without burning. It's both her secret weapon and old friend in helping create the paella's hallmark browned crust of yellow saffron rice. "I've had it for years," she says fondly. Only as deep as the first joint of her thumb with sloping sides, the pan's traditional design permits as much rice as possible to touch and crisp on the hot surface.

The iconic rice dish embodies Spain's history as a rich stew of

European, African and Arab influences. Rashida researched culinary lore for a radio show she once hosted. She says the word "paella" has roots in both the old French word for "pan" and the Arab for "leftovers." The Moorish kings introduced rice and saffron to Andalusia, and their servants created the dish from the remains of royal meals. Northern European invaders brought the round and shallow paella pan to the Iberian table.

Suddenly I'm back in my childhood kitchen where my mother is making "Spanish Rice"—a bland but hearty concoction of tomatoes, hamburger, and soft white rice—that stuck to the ribs of a growing family without much money. While Rashida loads her paella with vegetables spiked with hot peppers, mussels, clams, shrimp, prawns, octopus and squid, I think, *This, definitely, is not my mother's Spanish rice.*

Next comes the Andalusian white *gazpacho* or *ajoblanco.* "You can never have too much of a good thing ... or too much gazpacho," Spaniards say. To make the point, Rashida introduces me to an alternative to the well-known tomato-based version of the cold soup. It was prepared long before Columbus brought tomatoes from the new world. Together we whip up the silky emulsion of skinless almonds, milk, bread, garlic and sherry vinegar.

Finishing with a flourish of mascarpone mousse topped strawberry coulis, we savor our first meal, and it's difficult to leave the table. However, the afternoon wanes and my day's itinerary also calls for Rashida to show me "the charming and famous places" around Marbella, ending with a tapas dinner in a typical restaurant. I'm looking forward to the sights.

But after leaving her kitchen, Rashida seems to leave her competence behind. I become slightly uneasy when she takes the first wrong turn, then a second. Then a third. Fearing it's a trend, I pretend not to notice, telling myself it's her fatigue from the lingering effects of bronchitis, which has plagued her since my arrival. Eventually she crams her car into a too-small parking spot, and we reach Marbella's glorious beach just in time to watch the sky change from pink to black over the Mediterranean.

By the morning of our second day, Rashida's re-energized. Today we'll prepare red peppers stuffed with tuna, clams from Galicia, a carmelized apple tortilla—and my requested salt-baked fish.

"It's magic," if properly prepared, she says, then explains that as the salt hardens around the fish, it gently steams and seals in the juices. The skin, with its scales still intact, acts as a protective layer to keep the salt out and the seasonings in.

After stuffing the cavity of a three-pound pargo, a white-fleshed fish of the dorado family, with parsley and lemon, we cover it completely with a thick crust of coarse sea salt moistened with egg and flavored with fresh herbs and bake it in a very hot oven until the scent of salt and the sea fills the kitchen.

"When the crust turns yellow, the fish is cooked," Rashida says. With the concentration of a master *belloto* carver she cracks the crust with a spatula and brushes away the excess salt. As promised, the flesh pulls away from the bones, perfectly moist, seasoned—and not a bit salty.

Then come the two tapas. Rashida says, "tapas can be almost any food that counters the effects of alcohol during a night on the town," as long as it's a small serving. For us, these are *Almejas a la marinera*—clams sautéed in garlic, white wine and olive oil—a recipe from the northern province of Galicia; and red pimento stuffed with tuna, a dish from Catalonia.

For dessert our airy tortilla of carmelized apples and almonds is a recipe of Rashida's own design. "Spanish desserts are too heavy and sweet, so I create my own."

But once more we've stayed too long at table and cut short our sightseeing time. It's nearly five p.m. when we head to Casares, one of the many *pueblos blancos*, or white villages, that are stacked like sugar cubes on the mountains behind the Costa del Sol. Rashida finds her way without a map, but she gets lost in the town's one-lane streets, steep as ski jumps, looking to park. I ride shot-gun, helpless and ignored when I mention a sign that points the opposite direction to a parking lot. The whitewashed buildings lean in, squeezing us into a pedestrian alley where we can move neither forward nor back. Rashida finally dislodges the car with its side mirrors intact, but the parking process takes so much time we nearly miss the mountain-top castle ruins before dark.

For our final cooking session, we'll prepare spicy chicken stew with chorizo; sizzling prawns in garlic and hot peppers; and a flourless marzipan and chocolate cake. We begin with the stew. Fastidious about removing the fat, Rashida skins the legs, thighs and wings of a locally raised, organic chicken then browns them. The chicken simmers for an hour in wine and a rich chicken broth seasoned with onions, bay leaves and flakes of hot *guindilla* pepper. Rashida adds sweet red pepper slices and peas late in the cooking, because she "wants crunch. I like to see the vegetables," she explains. Wine, paprika, saffron and chorizo sausages made from a *belloto* pig finish the dish.

Meanwhile, *Gambas al Pil-Pil*—spicy prawns—sizzle in olive oil, garlic and hot pepper. I tease her about the fat content. "It's a tapa, a small plate; we don't eat much," Rashida rationalizes. Besides, our gluten-free marzipan and chocolate cake is made without butter or extra fat.

But when the time arrives for the afternoon excursion—a visit to a wine museum and tasting in the *pueblo blanco* Mijas—I gird myself.

Sure enough, the town encompasses three separate districts, and Rashida can't find the road signs toward the mountain.

We fly round the roundabouts.

"There's a sign for Mijas."

"No, that's for the beaches."

"No, it says Mijas Pueblo."

"No, we've already tried that turn."

By the time a lucky guess points us in the right direction, I'm dizzy, and the wine museum, along with almost everything else in town, has closed. Even the town's donkey taxis are heading to the barn. We look at the panoramic view of the Costa del Sol beaches, the Mediterranean far below, then head down only to lose our way back to Marbella.

On my last morning, I'm dubious when Rashida insists on taking me to my bus for Seville. "My son lives near the station; I pass it all the time," she assures me.

Reluctantly, I accept her ride. Sure enough, as if magnetized, Rashida gets sucked into another roundabout. After a couple of rotations, she breaks from its force field, asks directions which she doesn't follow, then backs the wrong way up a one-way street, pedestrians yelling and other drivers honking.

The fifteen-minute trip has taken forty-five. Fortunately, we started early, and yet another lucky turn reveals the station. With my well-fed stomach slightly queasy from the tumultuous ride, I say good-bye and board the bus.

Finally, as the rolling wheels lull me and my stomach settles, the follies of sightseeing with Rashida fade, but the taste of her fabulous meals, so lovingly prepared, lingers. No matter the wrong turns. It's been a delicious journey; Rashida has given me an invaluable roadmap to the cuisine of Andalusia. I imagine the spontaneous applause for my salt-crusted fish and seafood-laden paella from family and friends. The bumps in the road? As I relax and remember, they become funny adventures that actually spiced up the trip. They'll be the stories to laugh about and savor as much as any meal.

The Great Mosque at Córdoba

IN SEARCH OF A SHINING MOMENT
Anne Sigmon

We all call barbarous anything that is contrary to our own habits."
Michel de Montaigne, *The Compete Essays*

"We must learn to live together as brothers or perish together as fools."
Martin Luther King Jr., speech in St. Louis, March 22, 1964

The front page pictured a lifeless Syrian child, dusty limbs splayed in the gray rubble of Aleppo. As I looked up from *The New York Times*, my vision blurred with angry tears. That historic medieval city, and its children, had been reduced to a bombed-out flashpoint in the barbarous Syrian Civil War.

That was in May, 2013. Not much has changed since then. Sectarian violence still rages across the Middle East, much of it fueled by religious hate. The news still burns with images of dead children. Even after decades of savage bombings—from Baghdad to Aleppo to Istanbul; from New York to London, Madrid, Paris and Orlando—there seems no end. *How can we do that to each other?* I wondered. *To children? Why can't we be more tolerant?*

Perhaps Andalusia might hold a clue. These days, Spain seems just as fraught as the rest of the world with religious suspicion and intolerance. But it hadn't always been that way. Recently, as I was preparing for a trip there, I'd read about a magical time—a time when Muslims, Christians and Jews together created a glorious florescence of art, science and literature centuries ahead of the European Renaissance. The seat was the almost mythical al-Andalus—Andalusia.

A province of southern Spain today, from the eighth to the twelfth centuries Andalusia reigned as the world's most admired cultural center. It was ruled not by Western kings, but by a Muslim dynasty originally from Syria. Al-Andalus was the "ornament of the world" a medieval nun once wrote. That's also the title of a book I'd read by historian María Rosa Menocal. Reading the book, I wondered how a feudal society, often in conflict, achieved the kind of tolerance that eludes us today. I hoped to learn more during my visit.

A month later, I was there, in Andalusia, the land the Romans called Hispania. Wandering the ancient capital of Córdoba, I meandered across the Roman bridge built in the time of the Emperor Augustus, the first century CE. The old stone gleamed golden in the sun, glinting off the sixteen graceful arches that span the river Guadalquivir. A wisp of clouds drifted overhead in the sapphire-blue sky. I could almost imagine myself trailing the great Roman orator, Seneca the Elder, who was born and died in Córdoba, as he made his way across the eight-hundred-foot span. In his eighties, Seneca would have walked slowly, perhaps with a staff, laboring uphill toward the Roman Forum and the new Temple of Augustus. Imperial Rome worshipped the emperor like a god. But the Jews and early Christians in Andalusia were, nonetheless, free to practice their one-god religions, however peculiar they may have seemed to the Romans.

After Rome fell, the Visigoths ruled what was then called Hispania. At first the Goths—who practiced a liberal form of Christianity called

Arianism—were tolerant of the Jews. But after they embraced Catholicism in 589 CE, things turned ugly. Anti-Jewish decrees forbade Jews to marry Christian women. Jews were not allowed to own slaves—thus barring them from slave-dependent agriculture. In 613, the Visigoth king issued an edict that all Jews must be forcibly converted to Christianity.

I felt squeamish just reading about it. *Why was it so important that everyone share the same religion?* I've never understood that mindset.

As a symbol of their conversion, the Visigoths built a grand church—the Basilica of San Vicente—on a hill overlooking the Roman bridge. All that remains of San Vincente today are some pieces of mosaic floor, a carved stone sarcophagus, odd bit of scalloped stonework, and enigmatic crouching figures set into column bases.

The early persecution of the Jews in Spain ended, surprisingly, after a young Syrian prince escaped the overthrow and murder of his family—the Umayadds—in Damascus, hid in Morocco, and finally sailed across the Mediterranean in 755 CE to lead a vibrant new Muslim dynasty in Spain. His name was Abd al-Rahman. His dynasty, based in Córdoba, lasted for almost three hundred years.

By long tradition, Muslim rulers had allowed both Christians and Jews to practice their faiths. They were all "people of the book," followers of the one God of Abraham. At the beginning of al-Rahman's reign, the Muslims worshipped in the Christian basilica. But al-Rahman wasn't satisfied. History records his great longing—shared by his heirs and successors—to recreate the lost grandeur of the Umayyad Caliphate in Damascus. He bought the basilica from the Christians and, to replace it, started work on what he hoped would be the grandest mosque in all Islam. After seeing it for myself, I believe he succeeded.

The calming magic of the Great Mosque enveloped me as soon as I stepped over the threshold. In the hypostyle hall, a hypnotizing array of double horseshoe arches—vivid in alternating stripes of white stone and red brick—marched toward infinity. Yellow light radiated from lanterns that swung low in the dim hall. Scents of incense and earth drifted by, the mineral smells of great age. The enormous arches are lifted up, as if to heaven, by an army of 850 columns cut from veined marble, some gray, others red or green or white. Antique capitals perch atop the columns, some with delicately carved acanthus; others with broken palms. At 250,000 square feet, the space felt endless, a cavernous hymn to God. Sitting there, in the quiet, my own worries were reduced to specks of dust.

Many of the materials used to build the Great Mosque were reclaimed from Córdoba's past. Some of the capitals had their first use in the city's Roman temple; some marble columns graced the Visigothic Church of San Vicente—fragments of old faiths singing praises once more.

In al-Andalus, almost everyone spoke Arabic, the recognized language of art and science. In the ninth and tenth centuries, Córdoba was the jewel of Europe with a library system that was the envy the world. Scholars and booksellers flocked to the city. A tenth-century chronicler, whose name is lost to history, described Córdoba as "the highest of the high … the homeland of wisdom … the garden of the fruits of ideas."

To many historians, that was a golden age, a flourishing of spiritual and intellectual life. It's been called "*La Convivencia*"—coexistence— a time when Muslims, Christians and Jews lived in peace. Others say that idea is mere myth.

By all accounts, Muslim Spain was never an egalitarian society. Muslims, Christians and Jews lived side by side, yes. But Christians and Jews were second- and third-class citizens. Among other inequities, the government forced them to pay a "tribute tax" to practice their religions. There were "intractable differences and enduring hostilities," Menocal says in *Ornament of the World*. Yet "they were still able to nourish a culture of tolerance."

The political situation deteriorated over time. By the end of the tenth century the Muslim unity in al-Andalus had collapsed. The Iberian Peninsula had devolved into a constellation of small principalities, with Muslim states (called *taifas*) in the south and Christian states in the north, each striving to outdo the others. But alliances weren't necessarily drawn along religious lines. Muslim princes often allied with their Christian counterparts. Scholars, artists, poets and intellectuals of all faiths were in high demand to ornament the competing courts in distinctive Andalusian style. Despite the turbulent politics, the eleventh century was still a bright period of cultural achievement.

Then the light began to dim. In the twelfth century, fanatical Berber Muslims from Africa wrenched control from the Umayyads in Spain. The Berbers preached uncompromising jihad against Christians and Jews and, over time, stripped minorities of most of their rights.

Sitting in the courtyard of the old Córdoba synagogue, I imagine the chilling sight of ten thousand mounted men bearing down on me, their robes billowing with speed, heads swathed in white turbans, their faces masked by blue cloth scarves trailing behind them. I see only their fierce eyes and the sun glinting off the blade of a deadly scimitar. In the end, my only choices are: convert to Islam, escape the country, or die.

At about the same time, the crusade movement bred an equally zealous Christian ideology and a frenzied clamor for the *Reconquista* of lands lost to the Arabs. In 1212, the Catholic Pope Innocent III rallied European knights to a crusade in Spain. When it was over, Christian princes had conquered all of the Muslim principalities of al-Andalus except for small far-south redoubt in Granada.

The eerie parallels to our own twenty-first century conflicts made me shudder. *How little we've learned from history.* I thought of Syria and the glittering masterpieces of architecture that so inspired Abd al-Rahman. They stood as a beacon to civilization for two millennia. Now so many of them are lost, blown to rubble in the madness of the past five years.

After the *Reconquista* the Christian capital moved eighty-seven miles east to Seville. The Muslims were now the subjugated, many of them pushed south to Granada. Others stayed put in Christian-held areas. They acquired a name: *Mudéjar*, meaning unconverted Muslims who submitted to the rule of the Christian kings. It probably started as a slur, but later the term also defined the triumphant style of art and architecture that characterized the era—an exuberant fusion of gothic, Renaissance and Islamic form.

One of the most splendid achievements of *Mudéjar* art is the Réal Alcázar, the original Muslim fortress defending Seville. Over time, the Alcázar evolved into a royal palace, first for the Muslim princes and, later, their Christian successors.

Remarkably, even after the *Reconquista*, much of the old spirit of tolerance still survived to enrich Seville's culture. The Christian kings of the thirteenth century fostered a cosmopolitan court that encouraged learning. Jews, Muslims and Christians all had prominent roles.

A walk through Seville's Alcázar, especially in the late afternoon when the crowds are thin and the cicadas thrum, is more than a trek back in time; it's a magic carpet to another world, at once more brutal but in some ways more tolerant than our own. My favorite spot is the "new" palace, built by the Christian King Pedro I in 1364. Vibrant arabesque tiles and elaborate white plasterwork decorate nearly every inch of the interior walls.

Outside on the lovely Patio of the Maidens, I sat in a corner, on a low marble platform. Water burbled in a long rectangular pool surrounded by orange trees in fragrant bloom. Reflected in the water, the building's columns seemed to dance toward me. Tile stars shimmered as if they still hung in the sky. The breeze fluttered with the sounds of a dove calling, the flap of a bird's wing, a riff of Arabic music from someone's audio guide.

Arrayed among the stars, vines and flowers are cartouches in Arabic calligraphy that speak to the cultural integration of the palace's builders. My favorite: "In Praise of Allah and our Sultan Pedro." Other inscriptions: "Power belongs to Allah." "There is no victor but Allah." Allah. God. الله. The one God of all the people of the book.

On my visit to Andalusia, I'd hoped to learn how a great society of mixed religions lived in harmony for hundreds of years and produced one of history's greatest artistic cultures. Instead, I found that it was never that simple. That world was never harmonious. Still, even though there was almost constant conflict, long centuries of familiarity had softened religious extremism. Each community was willing to learn from the other.

Andalusia's long experiment in multicultural tolerance failed in the end. Medieval Spain eventually succumbed to a fanatic crusade mentality that gripped both sides. In this atmosphere of paranoia, the Jews and Muslims were expelled from Spain in 1492 by the Catholic Monarchs Ferdinand and Isabella. Al-Andalus, once the center of world culture and refinement, had lost its way.

Are we any different today? The radical hate that destroyed al-Andalus still rages around the world, particularly in Syria. The artistic patrimony of the original Umayyad civilization lies in ruins. Half a million Syrians have been killed. Half the population is homeless. Seven million people have fled the country and wander the globe, many of them unwelcome, in search of a new life. By the end of April 2014, the UN reported, almost nine thousand children had been killed in the war.

When I start to grow despondent about this, I try to think of al-Andalus. Stars still shine in the Alcázar. The art, and its message of tolerance, still speak to us—a tribute to the one God they all worshipped and a shining beacon of hope. Christians, Muslims and Jews found tolerance once. Perhaps, one day, we will find it again.

"I go into the Muslim mosque and the Jewish synagogue and the Christian church and I see one altar."

—Jalal ad-Din ar-Rumi, eleventh-century Sufi Muslim philosopher, *The Essential Rumi*

Spanish Oranges

BLOOD ORANGES

Joanna Biggar

—Inspired by *Un Été Impardonnable 1936: la guerre d'Espagne et la scandale de la non-intervention,* by Gilbert Grellet, Albin Michel, 2016

In Sevilla, in summer,
in 1936,
an Andalusian sun burns
in the July sky.

Bitter oranges
on the *naranjos amargos*
are already dead,
and
the generals come
one
by
one
by
one:
Quepo de Llano,

213

Juan Yagüe,
Francisco Franco.

A red moon rises
over Triana,
across the Guadalquivir,
where Carmen
dances
where
Carmen sings
for
her *caballero,*
her *toreador,*
her *amour.*
red dress flying
gypsy hips defying,
sangre de toro,
sangre de lágrimas,
sangre de Cristo.

In Triana,
at night,
the first blood runs
from
the throats
of children,
of grandmothers,
of seamstresses,
of workers,
of communists,
of gypsies,
of *caballeros,*

of *toreadors,*
of *amours,*
asleep in their beds.

When Carmen sings,
dances
the bloody streets—
red dress flying,
gypsy hips defying,
sangre de toro,
sangre de lágrimas,
sangre de Cristo—
a song is ripped
from the heart of
the *cantaor,*
"Grito de guerra, grito de Guerra
es un grito de Guerra."

The guitar strums
faster, faster, faster,
heels beating
ratatatatat
like castanets,
like gunfire,
like jackboots
ratatatatat
where the generals go next,
to Macarena,
to Casco Antiguo,
to Santa Cruz.
"Grito de Guerra, grito de guerra
Es un grito de guerra."

Still Carmen dances,
red dress flying
gypsy hips defying,
heels beating
ratatatatat
castanets,
gunfire,
jackboots
faster, faster, faster,
until
blood
breaks the banks
of the Guadalquivir.

Then
sangre de toro,
sangre de lágrimas,
sangre de Cristo,
the red tide
runs backwards
to Córdoba,
to Granada,
to Málaga
on the road
from Alsuería
to all of Spain.

Carmen twirls
red dress flying
gypsy hips defying,
castanets crying
like heels,

like gunfire,
like jackboots
ratatatatat.
And the *cantaor* is dying,
"Grito de guerra, grito de guerra
es un grito de guerra."

In Sevilla, in spring
in 1937,
the moon rises red
over Andalusia
where blood oranges,
naranjas de sangre,
now swing
from
naranjos amargos,
the bitter orange trees.

Beneath gunfire
skies,
the *cantaor* still cries
but
Carmen still dances,
Carmen still sings.

GLOSSARY

alegría	joy
almuerzo	lunch
bailarina	a dancer
banderillero	bullfighter who carries small flags
bercerrada	fight with young bulls
caballero	a gentleman
Caliphate	Muslim state in Spain ruled by Umayyad Dynasty, 756-1031 CE
cantaor	a singer
cante jondo	a vocal style of flamenco
casita	a small house
Chahar Bagh	a Persian-style garden layout in four parts
comestibles	groceries
Conversos	Jews who converted to Christianity
corrida de torros	a bullfight
duende	passion, inspiration, authenticity, soulfulness
estocada	act of thrusting sword

feria	a festival
finca	a farm
golpe!	to strike one's heel in flamenco dancing
grito	a cry
guerra	war
hammam	a steam bath or Turkish bath
hermandad	a brotherhood
jámon	ham
Mudéjar	Muslims in Spain after the *Reconquista*; popular art and architecture in the Moorish style of that period
muerte	death
naranjos amargos	bitter orange trees
naranjos de sangre	blood orange trees
paso	a float in a parade
pueblo	a town
raciones	large portions of food, often shared by many in a restaurant
sangre de toro	blood of the bull, a red wine popular in Spain
sangre de lágrimas	blood of tears

sangre de Cristo	blood of Christ
Semana Santa	Holy Week
Sevillanos	residents of Seville
taifas	small Muslim states in Spain
tienda	a store
toreador	term for bullfighter (French origin)
torero	term for bullfighter (Spanish origin)

AUTHOR BIOGRAPHIES

Tania Amochaev documents her world in the context of a past that never allowed her family the freedom to live for long in peace. Born in Belgrade, Serbia, of two displaced émigrés—a White Russian father and a Croatian mother—she spent her first years in a refugee camp before living a personal story of exile, asylum and success that America empowered. She watched, from afar, the disintegration of the country where her mother Zora's sisters ended on opposing sides of a battle, not for the first time. Fluent in the languages of her parents, she visits her homelands to inherit her past. In her book *Mother Tongue* she explores, in a highly personal saga, the causes and consequences of Balkan struggles over the last hundred years.

Tania, a writer, photographer, traveler, and successful technology executive, again lives in San Francisco, the city that offered her refuge when she was a child.

Her story about returning to her father's homeland was published in *Best Travel Writing*, Volume Ten. Her story about travel down the Ganges River will appear in Volume Eleven of that publication.

Unity Barry graduated from the San Francisco Art Institute, but after she worked for way too long in the corporate world, she retired to write about her favorite subjects—artists and Paris during the gilded age. She recently finished her first historical novel, *Luminous—Berthe Morisot and the Birth of Impressionism* and starting her next about Mary Cassatt. She was a short-listed finalist in the 2011 William Faulkner-William Wisdom Writing Competition and has two pieces in the anthology, *Wandering in Paris.*

Daphne Beyers grew up near Amish country in northeastern Pennsylvania, often finding herself caught in traffic behind wheel-and-buggy carriages. She's lived many places including London, New York City, San Francisco, Berkeley and Palm Springs. Daphne taught herself to program at the age of thirteen and works as a computer consultant for various Fortune 500 companies in the Bay Area. Her first essay, "Existential Cafe," was published in an award-winning anthology of Parisian stories, *Wandering in Paris: Luminaries and Love in the City of Light.* She has two essays in the anthology *Wandering in Cornwall,* where she recounts her adventures cycling through the Cornish countryside and her harrowing escape from the bird apocalypse. She currently lives north of San Francisco with a Scottish terrier who thinks he's a dragon.

Sandra Bracken made the first of many journeys alone to Peru where she walked the hills around Sacsayhuaman, photographed the stonework there and chartered a plane to fly over the lines at Nazca—all in the pursuit of art. She has a Master's Degree in Fine Fine Arts, taught drawing for twenty years and has exhibited sculpture and drawings in galleries and museums in the U.S. She collaborated on a collection of poems and collages, *Meet Me at the Wayside Body Shop,* and produced a chapbook of poems, *New Moon.* Travel stories were included in *Venturing in Ireland: Quest for the Modern Celtic Soul,*

Venturing in Italy: Puglia, Land between Two Seas and *Wandering in Paris: Luminaries and Love in the City of Light.* She lives in Maryland near her three children and five grandchildren. Her most recent travels have been with her husband—in pursuit of fish.

As the French child of a Jewish mother, **Antoinette Constable** witnessed atrocities inflicted on relatives, friends and strangers in Nazi-occupied France during WWII. She used this material to compile a chapbook of war-related poems, *The Lasting War,* published in December 2014. Antoinette has published numerous poems, four chapters of a novel, and prose pieces unrelated to the war. She's won a first poetry prize from PEN, an Ann Stanford award from SCA University, a month-long stay at a prestigious writers' retreat at Mesa Refuge in Point Reyes Station, California, and has contributed to the award-winning Wanderland Writers anthology, *Wandering in Paris: Luminaries and Love in the City of Light.* One of her poems served as inspiration for a Charleston Black Theatre production. Antoinette suffers headaches from not reading enough, enjoys puns, great food and friends, though not necessarily in this order.

Rita M. Gardner grew up as an expatriate in the Dominican Republic during a repressive dictatorship. Her award-winning memoir of that experience, *The Coconut Latitudes: Secrets, Storms, and Survival in the Caribbean,* was published in 2014 by She Writes Press. In 2015, it won two top national awards in the category of memoir. She is featured in *The Magic of Memoir*, a collection of inspirational stories and tips for memoir writers coming in fall 2016 by She Writes Press. Articles, poems and photographs have appeared in literary journals and travel magazines. Website and blog: www.ritamgardner.com

Donna Hemilla finds the best travel experiences arise from her inability to understand maps, even the electronic kind that talks to you. She inevitably turns left down narrow passageways when she should have gone straight. At those times, she thinks of her grandmother, Sophie, who left Poland at the age of 22 bound for America with $9 in her pocket and a desire only to see what was waiting around the next bend. Hint: It will always be something amazing you didn't expect. Donna has worked as a news reporter, business editor and speechwriter. She lives in Berkeley, California, and writes children's books.

Laurie McAndish King still smells like chocolate. Her book of travel stories, *Lost, Kidnapped, Eaten Alive! True Stories from a Curious Traveler*, was published in 2014. Laurie's award-winning essays and photography have appeared in *Smithsonian* magazine, the *San Francisco Chronicle*, *The Best Women's Travel Writing*, *The Sun* literary journal, and other magazines and literary anthologies. She also wrote *An Erotic Alphabet* and co-edited, along with Linda Watanabe McFerrin, two volumes of erotica in the *Hot Flashes: sexy little stories and poems* series. Laurie has an undergraduate degree in philosophy and a master's degree in education, and enjoys gardening and taxidermy. She lives in northern California. www.LaurieMcAndishKing.com

Thanasis Maskaleris was born in Arkadia, Greece, and immigrated to the U.S. at the age of 17. He has written original poetry in Greek and in English, and has translated contemporary Greek poetry and prose extensively.

He taught Comparative Literature and Modern Greek Literature at San Francisco State University where he was the Founding Director of the Center for Modern Greek Studies and spearheaded the establishment of the Nikos Kazantzakis Chair. One of his recent publications (co-edited/translated with Nanos Valaoritis) is *An Anthology of Modern Greek Poetry.*

Most recently he published *The Terrestrial Gospel of Nikos Kazantzakis—Will the Humans Be Saviors of the Earth?*—an anthology of passages about nature, hymns to the earth intended to inspire ecological action. Thanasis also published *My Life on the Ragged Paths of Pan—Selected Poems and Translations.*

Gayle McGill grew up in St. Catharines, Ontario, with four brothers in a poor but high-spirited family. She came of age in the sixties, and after graduating from McMaster University, spent her young adult years carting an enormous backpack around the globe. Her love of travel has not diminished. She has been identified as a tree hugger, music lover, science wonderer and one that worries way too much about feminist issues. Her work career has been long and varied— teacher, barmaid, travel agent, and for the last three decades, programmer. She is the author of a novel set in the Australian Outback, and many technical "How To" guides. Gayle has written thousands of lines of code that live on in software systems all over the Bay Area. Her code has won acclaim and has been translated into other languages. Oakland has been her home for the past thirty years where she lives with her belligerent garden and amicable husband John and daughter Anna nearby.

Mary Jean Pramik, a coalminer's daughter and a great, great-granddaughter of the Mongolian plane, has hitchhiked across the United States, tracked May Apples in Ohio, chased children through wet mountains of California, fended off bill collectors in tropical San Francisco, and counted sharp-talon bird carcasses along the Pacific's Point Reyes sands. Communicating with screeching penguin hoards in Antarctica remains a high point of her sojourn on this planet. MJ

226

Pramik earned undergraduate and graduate degrees in biological sciences, and completed an MFA in Writing. She moonlights as a medical writer, penning such scientific thrillers as *Norenthindrone, The First Three Decades*, the fast-paced history of the first birth control pill extracted from a Mexican yam. Winner of the coveted Mary Womer Medal and a Travelers' Tales Solas Award, MJ Pramik's articles and essays have appeared in *Nature Biotechnology, Drug Topics,* and *Cosmetic Surgery News*, and mainstream publications such as *Good Housekeeping, Odyssey*, and the *National Enquirer*. She has contributed to the "*Venturing in*" travel series on the Canal du Midi, Southern Greece, Southern Ireland, and Puglia, Italy, and the "*Wandering in*" series for Costa Rica, Bali, Paris and Cornwall. She teaches graduate writing skills in the College of Science and Engineering at San Francisco State University.

Lynne Rutan isn't sure whether it was in the marbled luxury of San Francisco's Fairmont Hotel or amid the natural splendor of the Grand Tetons, but somewhere during a cross-country trip with her grandparents when she was thirteen, the travel bug bit—hard—and she's still scratching the itch four decades later. While living in New York City she worked all over the world for the American Society of Travel Agents and other travel industry companies and freelanced for travel trade magazines and the *New York Daily News*. Six years in Brussels gave her the opportunity to explore Europe and fueled her passion for cooking and culinary tourism. She discovered another passion, hiking, during a four-day adventure to Machu Picchu and has since trekked in Tasmania, New Zealand, Tibet, Canada and the mountains that surround her home in Park City, Utah.

Anne Sigmon flunked jump rope in seventh grade and washed out of college PE. After college, she headed for San Francisco and a career in public relations. Exotic travel was the stuff of dreams until, at 38, she married Jack, took tea with erstwhile headhunters in Borneo and climbed Mt. Kilimanjaro at 43. Five years later, she was zapped by a career-ending stroke caused by an obscure autoimmune disease called Antiphospholipid Syndrome (APS). She may be stuck with blood thinners and a damaged brain, but she's still traveling to isolated regions ranging from Botswana to Burma and, most recently, to Syria, Jordan, and a remote rainforest in Costa Rica. Anne's personal essays and travel stories have appeared in local and national publications including *Good Housekeeping* and *Stroke Connection* magazines and the anthologies *Wandering in Costa Rica, Chicken Soup for the Soul: Find Your Happiness,* and *Travel Stories from Around the Globe.* She is currently working on a memoir about her experience with stroke and autoimmune disease. Anne's blog www.JunglePants.com offers travel tales and tips about adventure travel off the beaten path. On her author website, www.AnneSigmon.com, she writes about—and offers tips on—living with stroke and autoimmune disease.

Maryly Snow is an Oakland-born visual artist once known for her 1979 installation *An Act of Bad Taste By a Woman Raised for Impeccability.* This garnered her her Warholian fifteen minutes of fame via a news clip on a local San Francisco television station and an invitation to appear on *Good Morning America.* These days she is primarily a printmaker with etchings in the Library of Congress, the Fine Arts Museum of San Francisco, the University of California, Berkeley, and many corporate and private collections. As an art and architecture visual librarian at UC Berkeley (remember 35mm slides?) before she retired in 2007, Maryly published many papers, winning the Nancy DeLaurier Writing Award in 2000 for her briefly titled essay "Pedagogical Consequences of Photomechanical Reproduction in the Visual Histories: From Copy Photography to Digital Mnemonics" in *Visual Resources* 12:3-4, 1996 (double issue

entitled, *Copyright, Fair Use and the Great Image Debate*). More recently, she was the editor of the award-winning book *California Society of Printmakers: One Hundred Years, 1913-2013*, currently undergoing conversion to an e-book. Maryly's West Oakland studio is open by appointment.
www.snowstudios.com

EDITOR BIOGRAPHIES

Joanna Biggar
is a teacher, writer and traveler whose special places of the heart include the California coast and the South of France. She has degrees in Chinese and French and, as a professional writer for thirty years, has written poetry, fiction, personal essays, features, news and travel articles for hundreds of publications including *The Washington Post Magazine, Psychology Today, The International Herald Tribune,* and *The Wall Street Journal.* Her book *Travels and Other Poems* was published in 1996, and her most recent travel essays have appeared in the Wandering series, whose anthologies include books on Costa Rica, Bali, Paris and Cornwall. A novel, *That Paris Year,* was published by Alan Squire Publishing in 2010 and she is working on two sequels. She has taught journalism, creative writing, personal essay and travel writing in many venues, and has juried the annual awards for the Northern California chapter of the Society of Professional Journalists. She serves on the Board of Directors of Emiliano Zapata Street Academy in Oakland, California, where she makes her home, and is a longtime member of the Society of Woman Geographers. Contact her through email (jobiggar@gmail.com), Facebook at That Paris Year, or her blog, www.joannabiggar.org.

Linda Watanabe McFerrin (www.lwmcferrin.com) is a poet, travel writer, novelist and contributor to numerous newspapers, magazines and anthologies. She is the author of two poetry collections, past editor of a popular Northern California guidebook and a winner of the Katherine Anne Porter Prize for Fiction. Her novel, *Namako: Sea Cucumber*, was named Best Book for the Teen-Age by the New York Public Library. In addition to authoring an award-winning short story collection, *The Hand of Buddha*, she has co-edited twelve anthologies, including the *Hot Flashes: sexy little stories & poems* series. Her latest novel, *Dead Love* (Stone Bridge Press, 2009), was a Bram Stoker Award Finalist for Superior Achievement in a Novel.

Linda has judged the San Francisco Literary Awards, the Josephine Miles Award for Literary Excellence and the Kiriyama Prize, served as a visiting mentor for the Loft Mentor Series and been guest faculty at the Oklahoma Arts Institute. A past NEA Panelist and juror for the Marin Literary Arts Council and the founder of Left Coast Writers®, she has led workshops in Greece, France, Italy, England, Ireland, Central America, Indonesia, Spain and the United States and has mentored a long list of accomplished writers and best-selling authors toward publication.

CPSIA information can be obtained
at www.ICGtesting.com
Printed in the USA
FSOW02n1536181116
27411FS